SILENT TEACHINGS *of* MEHER BABA
DISCOURSES AND CONVERSATIONS

Published by Beloved Archives, Inc.,
a non-profit tax-exempt corporation,
599 Edison Drive,
East Windsor, New Jersey 08520, USA

Towards the production of this book,
selfless assistance rendered by Sunil Arora with tangible support to our library
project, Kendra Crossen-Burroughs for copyediting, Trish Sports towards
production and Tracy Floyd for book design. Our gratitude.

For information on the life, work and teachings of Meher Baba, write:
Naosherwan Anzar
Beloved Archives, Inc.
599 Edison Drive
East Windsor, New Jersey 08520, USA

Library of Congress Cataloging in Publication Data: 2001 132545

ISBN: 0 - 9702396 - 1 - 0
PRINTED IN THE UNITED STATES OF AMERICA

SILENT TEACHINGS

of

MEHER BABA

DISCOURSES AND CONVERSATIONS

~

COMPILED *and* EDITED
by NAOSHERWAN ANZAR

*B*eloved *A*rchives, Inc.

SILENT TEACHINGS *of* MEHER BABA

Excerpts from the Discourses of Meher Baba

⌒ CONTENTS ⌒

∼ FOREWORD ∽

SILENT TEACHINGS OF MEHER BABA is a sharing of words to live by—words that transform consciousness, words that awaken. The book is a revised edition of two short works that have been out of print for some years. The first is a collection of discourses originally titled Silent Revelations of Meher Baba: Excerpts from the Silent Discourses of Meher Baba, compiled, edited, and published in 1944 by Alexander Markey, a Hollywood screenwriter. The content was drawn from discourses given out by Baba in the 1930s and edited by C. D. Deshmukh. Meher Baba had given Markey permission to rework the material into a series of short discourses for Western readers. The present version is now republished by Beloved Archives with minor editorial corrections.

The second work is based on Meher Baba's exchanges with disciples and seekers from England, Europe, and America who contacted him in the thirties, and whose interviews were meticulously recorded by F. H. Dadachanji (Baba's first secretary, known as Chanji) and Princess Norina Matchabelli. From their diaries I compiled the conversations that were originally published in 1972 by the Glow Publications under the title The Answer: Conversations with Meher Baba. This work is now reissued in a slightly revised version.

We thus have, in a single volume, two aspects of Meher Baba's messages given in words: one in the more formal shape of written discourses, the other in the more personal give and take of face-to-face exchange. In both cases, Baba's words were given (by means of his alphabet board) out of the silence he had undertaken beginning on July 10, 1925. When Meher Baba first declared his intention to observe silence, his disciples asked him, "If you keep silence, how will you teach us?" To this question, he replied, "I have come not to teach, but to awaken." Meher Baba, the Avatar of the age—that same Ancient One who has come again to redeem humanity from the grip of illusion—thus expressed in a nutshell his great mission of arousing humanity from the sleep of ignorance and illusion, into consciousness of its inherent divinity.

Meher Baba offered a succinct statement of the origin and purpose of his ministry in September 1931 to Mohandas K. Gandhi, the leader of India's independence movement, who was a fellow passenger on the ship that brought Baba to the West for the first time. Gandhi had requested a meeting with Baba and had asked him: Can we form an idea of the experience [of bliss] from your explanation? Meher Baba replied:

> *It is all to be felt, seen, and realized. Words fail to give an idea. But for you I will relate my experience as to what I felt and saw when I first got it. After the year 1911, while I was studying in Deccan College for Inter Arts [in Pune], I used to frequently pass by a holy lady called Babajan who had her seat beneath a neem tree. One day, I just stopped by to see her, feeling instinctively drawn towards her. Our eyes met and she beckoned me to come nearer; when I approached her, she gave me a warm kiss and embrace. That divine touch and embrace made me forget all mental existence, and I passed through a divine thrill and an indescribable experience as if electric sparks from a battery with million of tiny sparks were shooting from my frame. Thereafter, although physically fit, I could not eat and sleep for nine months. My parents made me undergo different treatments for bringing on sleep, but to no avail. I was thereafter instinctively guided to go to Upasani Maharaj for the remainder of my work, that is, to bring back the normal state of consciousness. It took me nine years to get it back, and within that period I was made to undergo such training and experiences that all this is illusion and that there is only One Infinite Existence: I find myself in everything and every-one. And now it is my mission in life to impart this Experience and Knowledge to all who come and seek it.*

How did Meher Baba intend to accomplish the work of imparting this divine knowledge and awareness? Early on it was evident that this realization would come about through the force of his divine love. "I have come to sow the seed of love in your hearts," he declared, "so that in spite of all superficial diversity which your life in illusion must experience and endure, the feeling of oneness through love is brought about amongst all nations, creeds, sects, and castes of the world."

Yet, while Meher Baba's work is to help people realize the Self through love, the words that issued spontaneously from his silence were undoubtedly one important vehicle for that love. Meher Baba attaches a powerful spiritual energy to his words, which thus have the ability to awaken and transform all those who hear and read them.

In the discourses in this book, Meher Baba, often with great forcefulness, shows the practical way towards direct work on oneself, points out the pitfalls on the spiritual path, and provides means for a better understanding of the inner conditions that are indispensable on the pathway to God-realization. In the conversations, with gentle and loving advice, he opens the hearts of his listeners to intuitive receptivity. One of Meher Baba's English disciples, Charles Purdom, who was present for a number of interviews such as the ones presented here, observed that "Meher Baba's constant endeavor in each interview is to arouse confidence in the heart of the questioner. He will not permit depression to continue, he drives away fears, he says there is nothing to worry about. Many of the questions are asked by those who want to 'understand,' usually something about themselves. Meher Baba's answer invariably is not to think more, but to act, to do the simplest thing, for understanding comes from action. The confidence he seeks to arouse is in the heart, it is not intellectual conviction — about that he is indifferent. He wants people to feel." It is in this spirit that Beloved Archives offers this publication.

One small note about the editing of these discourses: Readers will notice the frequent usage of masculine nouns and pronouns to denote both men and women. Meher Baba's teachings were not intended to convey a male bias, and elsewhere he has clearly stated: "Since male and female incarnations are equally necessary for Self-knowledge, it is not right to look upon one as being more important than the other." Nonetheless, in order to keep alterations to a minimum and for the sake of historical accuracy, it was decided to retain the language conventions of the time in which these writings were first prepared.

Naosherwan Anzar
East Windsor
New Jersey, USA
2001

⁓ THE QUEST ⁓

CONSCIOUSLY OR UNCONSCIOUSLY, every living creature seeks one thing. In the lower forms of life and in less advanced human beings, the quest is unconscious; in advanced human beings it is conscious. The object of the quest is called by many names: happiness, peace, freedom, truth, love, perfection, Self-realization, God-realization, union with God. Essentially it is a search for all of these, because all of these and all other noble concepts, no matter what their name, turn out in the end to be one. Everyone has moments of happiness, glimpses of truth, fleeting experiences of affinity with God; what everyone longs for is to make them permanent.

It is a natural desire, based fundamentally on a memory, dim or clear as the individual's evolution may be low or high, of his essential unity with God; for all living creatures are partial manifestations of God, conditioned only by their lack of knowledge of their own true nature. The whole of evolution is in fact a progression from unconscious divinity to conscious divinity, in which God Himself, essentially eternal and unchangeable, assumes an infinite diversity of forms, passes through an endless variety of experiences, and transcends a countless number of self-imposed limitations.

Evolution from the standpoint of the Creator is a divine sport, in which the unconditioned tests the infinitude of His absolute knowledge, power, and bliss in the midst of all conditions. But evolution from the standpoint of the creature, with his limited knowledge, limited power, and limited capacity for enjoying bliss, is an epic of alternating rest and struggle, joy and sorrow, love and hate, until in the perfected man God balances the pairs of opposites and transcends duality. Then creature and Creator recognize themselves as one; changelessness is established in the midst of change, eternity is experienced in the midst of time. God knows Himself as God, unchangeable in essence, infinite in manifestation, ever experiencing the supreme bliss of Self-realization in continually fresh awareness of Himself by Himself.

The realization must and does take place only in the midst of life, for it is only in the midst of life that limitation can be experienced and transcended, and subsequent freedom from limitation can be enjoyed. Such is the quest — the inner driving urge of the soul — that has saved man again and again from total moral disintegration, and that will eventually lead him through ignorance, awakening, and illumination, to ultimate spiritual redemption. My function is to indicate the direction of the path that man has to travel, point out the pitfalls on the way, lessen the hazards of the difficult passages, and lighten and ease the final lap that ends in the culmination of his quest.

I bring to man divine love and the life eternal.

⌒ WAR AND BEYOND ⌒

WAR AND THE SUFFERING THAT IT INEVITABLY BRINGS cannot be avoided by mere propaganda against war. If war is to disappear from human experience, it is essential to destroy its root cause. The life of illusory values in which man is self-caught is the breeding ground for the chaos that precipitates war; individual and collective egoism and selfishness, which hold most of mankind in their thrall, are its root cause.

Man alone is responsible for war; through greed, vanity, selfishness, and cruelty, he brings the recurring evil of it upon himself. God, in His grace, transmutes this man-wrought tragedy into a channel for the quickening of humanity to a concept of higher values. Appalling and devastating though it is, war is thus saved by the Infinite from remaining an unmitigated evil.

To purge himself, man has to become conscious of the redeeming God-design in man-created war. To understand the real significance of violence and nonviolence in this God-transmuted pattern of spiritual values requires a true perception of the meaning and purpose of existence. Man's actions in war, therefore, should not be motivated by slogans, however high-sounding, that are based on erroneous concepts of violence or nonviolence; his actions require the prompting of spiritual understanding, which is above man-made rules, and of divine love, which is above man-conceived duality.

God's design infuses man's war with the capacity to generate and foster many qualities of divine importance, thus preventing it from being wholly without spiritual significance. When man's mania for possessions and dominance forces a peaceful nation or people to take up arms for the sake of higher values, for unselfish considerations of general well-being, war becomes not merely inevitable, but spiritually defensible.

Under the stress of imminent danger, war inspires behavior that is free from the limited self and action kindled by the impersonal spirit of willing sacrifice and suffering for the safety and welfare of others. It is better that such unselfish qualities be at least partially released under the stimulus of danger than that they remain wholly dormant; it is preferable for the pressure of collective calamity to free man — if only temporarily — from his petty self than for him to remain permanently enslaved by the ignoble pursuit of personal safety and the ruthless perpetuation of his selfish interests and existence.

In war, people are roused to make unlimited sacrifices and endure untold agony for the sake of their countries or principles. In doing so, they demonstrate their capacity for similar or even greater sacrifice and endurance for yet higher stakes: for the triumph of the soul.

War reveals that even the man in the street can rise to the greatest heights of sacrifice for the sake of a selfless cause. It also teaches that all worldly things — wealth, possessions, power, fame, family, the very tenor of life upon this earth — are transitory and devoid of lasting worth. The soul-searing incidents of war are enriched by the divine endowment to teach man lessons that will ultimately win him over to God, lessons that have the power to initiate him into a new life inspired by God-Truth and founded on imperishable spiritual values. If man fails to learn these divine lessons of war and to profit by them, he will have suffered and died in vain.

To claim special dispensation in war for any particular race, religion, or ideology is indefensible. All such assertions are based on the false doctrine of division and duality. Since the law of the universe is synonymous with oneness, and oneness precludes soul-separation of one individual from another, there is no justification whatsoever for any one side in war to claim that God favors it exclusively. God does not scale His grace to suit man's temporal quarrels and prejudices. His favor knows no discrimination, for His love is all-embracing.

The time has come for man to acquire a new vision and to proclaim the ultimate truth that all life is one; that all life merges in God, who is the only Reality; that God alone is worth dying for and living for; that all else is a vain and empty pursuit of illusory values.

The spiritual oneness of all souls remains inviolate in spite of war; and from the point of view of ultimate Reality, no soul is ever actually at war with any other soul. War is a conflict between different ideologies and concepts, which extends to and involves not only the minds but also the bodies of people; but the undivided and indivisible *soul* of mankind remains one in its unimpeachable and integral unity. The divine catalyst that keeps the oneness of all souls in creation intact, even in the midst of the most devastating war, is love.

All collective efforts draw upon some aspect of love for their functioning, and wars are no exception. They too are often motivated and conducted by a form of love; but it is a love whose nature has not been understood. For even though wars demand the large-scale organizing and functioning of cooperative endeavor, the spiritual potential of such a collective undertaking is artificially restricted by identification with segregated groups or limited ideals.

In order for love to come into its own, it must be freed from all impediments and released from all limitations. Love manifests in all phases of human life but is restricted to and often poisoned by personal ambition, racial pride, narrow loyalties, individual and national rivalries, chauvinism, and attachment to caste, sect, religion, or sex. To usher in the resurrection of humanity, the heart of man will have to be unlocked and a new love generated in it: the love that knows no limitation or corruption, the ultimate love that is wholly free from individual and collective greed.

Only through such a universal interflow of selfless love will it be possible for humanity to eradicate greed, intolerance, and exploitation—the three demons responsible for war—in all the gross and subtle forms that they assume in civilized life. In no other way can the mass mind be purged of the age-old psychosis of war; through no other means can it perceive with redeeming clarity that war is not merely abominable but in truth *never* necessary as a means of adjusting differences of *any* kind between nations. The chief task of those deeply concerned with the regeneration of humanity is to wage a holy war against the pernicious state of mind that justifies aggression in any form. This can be accomplished only by dispelling the spiritual apathy and ignorance that hold the mass of mankind in bondage.

If humanity is to redeem itself, it will have to emerge from the dreadful cataclysm of war with unimpaired spiritual integrity; with hearts free from the poison of malice and revenge; with minds disburdened of blows given and received; with souls unscathed by suffering and filled with the spirit of unconditional surrender to the divine will that is to inspire and ensoul the New Humanity.

⌒ THE NEW HUMANITY ⌒

To DIAGNOSE THE PROBLEM OF MANKIND as merely the problem of bread is to reduce humanity to the level of animality. However, even in the limited field of purely material adjustment, man cannot succeed unless he approaches his problems with spiritual understanding.

Material adjustment is but part of the wider problem of spiritual adjustment. Spiritual adjustment requires the elimination of the self, not only from the material aspects of life, but also from the spheres affecting intellectual, emotional, cultural, social, and political life.

Thus, in the hour of trial, let not our thoughts be for our limited selves, but for others; let us not be prompted by our egos, but responsive to the claims of our *divine* selves, which unite us with the rest of mankind. We cannot dodge our responsibility by evasion. To ignore human suffering as merely an illusory aspect of the illusory universe is indefensible. Not by ignoring suffering but by ministering to it with creative love do we gain the road to life eternal. Not through aloofness or indifference, but by eager selfless service are we brought nearer the fountain-source of that transcendental rhythm which is at the heart of God's universe.

Service with reservations is mere window dressing. In identifying ourselves with a narrow group or faction, or with some limited ideal, we do not achieve a real fusion of our segregated selves, only the appearance of such fusion. The true merging of the limited self with the ocean of universal life involves the complete surrender of isolated existence in all its aspects.

Foggy conjecture or a hodgepodge of stale ideas is no substitute for a clear definition of man's true goal. If the world culture of tomorrow is to be an improvement on the savagery of today, it will have to emerge from an absolute understanding of the universal law, wholly independent of existing traditions and superstitions; it will not come into being through the sterile process of disembalming and rehashing obsolete values.

The glorious vista of God's cosmic plan is obscured by creeds, dogmas, sectarianism, and superstitions. These limitations can be transcended by man not by blindly denying that there is any worth in existing concepts, but by discovering, unfolding, accentuating, and developing whatever fragments of divine truth may be hidden in them. This, however, must be accomplished not within narrow, rigid limits, but in an atmosphere of pure, unhampered love. Such love cannot function in an environment polluted by prejudice of any kind.

Humanity—kindness and compassion toward all created beings—is the real test of civilization. The true barbarian is one who is devoid of humanity. Though a man be a learned master of science or a paragon of worldly attainment, if he lacks humanity he is still a barbarian.

In every part of the world, people are perpetually disintegrating into narrow groups based on the superficial and essentially false differences of caste, creed, race, nationality, religion, ideology, or culture. Since these groups have long been accustomed to distrusting and fearing those outside their self-imposed boundaries, they are animated by indifference, contempt, or hostility toward each other. This attitude is born of ignorance, prejudice, envy, and selfishness; it can be remedied only by fostering a spirit of mutuality, which breaks through artificial isolationism and derives its imperishable strength from the sense of the inviolable unity of life as a whole. Love alone can achieve this. Spontaneous love, which knows no man-created boundaries, is the great universal bond that unites all living creatures in the immortal oneness of soul-identity.

Spontaneous love is not born of mere determination; through the exercise of will, one can at best be dutiful. With effort and persistence, one may succeed in bringing this sense of duty into conformity with one's pet concept of what is right; but such action is spiritually barren because it lacks the inner beauty of voluntary love. Love has to spring spontaneously from within; it is in no way amenable to outer compulsion. Love and coercion are incompatible; but though love cannot be forced upon anyone, it may be awakened through love itself.

Love is essentially self-communicative; those blessed with love may fructify others who are devoid of it. True love is unconquerable and irre-sistible; it goes on gathering power and spreading itself, until eventually it ennobles everyone and everything it touches.

Once it is universally recognized that there are no claims greater than the claims of the universal divine life, which includes all beings and all things without exception, this pure interflow of immaculate love not only will create lasting peace, harmony, and happiness in individual, national, and international spheres, but will shine forth in its own purity and beauty as God's most precious gift to man.

The New Humanity will come into being through the release of selfless love in measureless abundance. Through the free, unhampered interplay of true love from heart to heart, man will attain the new state of being, the highest level of life destined for him upon this earth.

Divine love is impervious to the onslaughts of duality, for it is an expression of Godhood—Infinite Unity—itself. Through divine love, the New Humanity will be brought in tune with the holy plan. Divine love will not merely usher in imperishable kindness among individuals and infinite bliss in personal life, but will also make possible the flowering of harmonious cooperative life among the peoples of the world. It will give birth to an era in which mankind will be emancipated from the tyranny of dead forms, an age that will give full scope to the creative life, bringing spiritual illumination to man's inspiration. It will be an era free from illusion, rooted in divine Reality; an age blessed with lasting peace and abiding happiness; the millennium that will initiate man into the life of eternity.

The New Humanity calls for creative statesmanship that will recognize and emphasize this great potentiality of mankind, a leadership that is dynamically aware of the essential unity of all human beings, not only through their predestined co-partnership in the Divine Plan for man upon earth, but also by virtue of the fact that they are all living expressions of the one life.

No line of action—no covenant—will be helpful or fruitful unless it is in absolute harmony with this profound law of the universe. The regeneration of humanity depends upon leadership with the wisdom to understand this transcendental fact, the inspiration to make creative use of it, and the authority to put it into operation.

⌁ MAYA: CREATOR OF ILLUSION ⌁

ALL HUMAN BEINGS, whether they are conscious of it or not, want to realize the ultimate Truth; but Truth cannot be known and realized as *Truth* unless ignorance is known and realized as *ignorance*; it is therefore of vital importance that man understand Maya, the principle of ignorance in creation. To understand Maya is to know half the Truth of the universe. It is imperatively necessary for man to know what is false, for unless he knows it, he cannot get rid of it; and rid himself of it he must, if he is to achieve spiritual redemption.

The apparent existence of the duality of a God *Infinite* and a world *finite* is illusory; for in infinitude there is truly no room for anything else or anyone else. How, then, does the false world of finite phenomena come into existence? It is created by Maya.

Maya eludes the comprehension of the finite mind; its very existence depends on eluding it. For if the finite mind of man could readily grasp the meaning of Maya, the whole intricate scheme of deception—which is Maya's stock-in-trade, with which it has held all of mankind in its grip from time immemorial—would instantly disintegrate; it would in fact have been unable to hoodwink man in the first place. So it is in the very nature of Maya to have placed itself beyond the pale of the human mind. In whatever manner the limited intellect tries to understand or explain Maya, it falls short of the truth. Maya is as unfathomable as God; Maya is God's shadow. While both God and Maya are beyond the comprehension of the limited intellect functioning in the world of duality, they come to be thoroughly understood in the clear light of spiritual realization. Not until then is the enigma of Maya completely and finally solved for man.

Maya itself is not illusion; it is the creator of illusion. Maya is not false; it is that which creates false impressions. Maya is not unreal; it is that which makes the real appear unreal and the unreal appear real. Maya is not duality; it is that which causes duality.

Maya becomes irresistible by taking possession of the very seat of knowledge—the human intellect. Maya is difficult to surmount, because under its sway the intellect—so dear to man—creates and upholds false beliefs and illusions with insidious logic that on the surface seems the last word in wisdom. The intellect that functions in freedom prepares the way and assists the aspirant in the realization of the divine Truth; but the intellect that is a slave to Maya, concentrates all its vast capacity and cunning on preventing true understanding.

Falsehood consists in taking the true as being false or the false as being true: in other words, considering anything to be other than what it intrinsically is. Mistakes in valuation can be committed in three ways: taking as important that which is unimportant; taking as unimportant that which is important; and attributing to something an importance that is other than its true significance. All these falsehoods are creations of Maya.

The value of sense objects is great or small according to the intensity or urgency of the individual's lusts and longings. They have *potential* value when the lusts or longings are *latent*; they assume *actual* value when they become active. But every one of these values is false; for when ultimately all lusts and longings disappear, these pseudo-values are stripped of their borrowed importance and stand naked in their true light: empty, unreal deceptions.

A characteristic example of attributing importance to what is un-important is the prevalent attitude toward death. The death of a loved one usually arouses feelings of sorrow and loneliness. This sense of grief for the deceased, whom one had been accustomed to seeing so often in the flesh, is, however, rooted in attachment to the *form* of the departed, not the *soul*. In his ignorance, man is not aware that even though the form—the outer garment—has vanished, the soul is not dead; in fact it has not even passed away, because the soul is imperishable, ever-present, everywhere. The feeling of loneliness, the lingering memory of the beloved, the longing for his or her presence, the tears of bereavement and sighs of separation—all are due to false valuation; they are the product of Maya.

Few are interested in God for His own sake. If the worldly-minded turn to God at all, it is mostly for their own selfish, mundane purposes. They seek gratification of their cravings, hopes, through the intervention of a god of their own conceit—or a deity who is the special fabrication and exclusive monopoly of the church or cult to which they happen to belong.

They do not seek God to satisfy an inner hunger for spiritual Truth. They long for all things except the only Truth, which they ignore as wholly unimportant. They pursue happiness through everything except the Truth of God, the only unfailing source of abiding joy. This distortion of man's vision in which the important is considered unimportant is also a device of Maya.

An example of giving an importance to a thing other than its intrinsic significance occurs when rituals, ceremonies, and other routine religious practices are regarded as ends in themselves. They have their own value as means of expression, as vehicles of spiritual conditioning, but as soon as they are permitted or encouraged to assume claims in their own right, they are invested with an importance that does not belong to them and to which they have no rightful claim. When thus clothed by Maya with an importance beyond their true measure, they bind and atrophy life rather than quicken and help unfold it.

False beliefs, too, are among the tricks Maya uses to hold the soul in ignorance and bondage. The false beliefs created by Maya are so deep-rooted and powerful that they assume in the average consciousness the status of self-evidence. They masquerade in the garb of veritable truths and are accepted by the mass of mankind without question.

For example, man believes that what he is, is represented by his physical body. It never occurs to him that he might be something other than what seems embodied in his tangible form. Identification with the body is accepted by him instinctively, without further proof. All his mundane senses and his ego-mind constantly attest what he has always regarded as an incontrovertible "fact"; and he holds the belief all the more strongly because he is so sure of his premise that he needs no further rational proof to support it.

To give up the belief that he is the body would involve the renunciation of all his desires pertaining to the physical body and all the false values spawned by them. That is why the belief that he is his physical body becomes natural to man; it is easy to hold and difficult to uproot. By contrast, belief that man is something other than his physical body seems unnatural, calling for convincing proof; this belief is difficult to hold and easy to resist. Yet, when the mind is ultimately freed of all physical desires and attachments, the belief that man is his physical body proves to be utterly false, and the revelation that he is something wholly other than his physical body emerges as the truth. This is equally true of man's subtle and mental bodies.

Man cherishes his false beliefs because he has come to relish them. Maya has succeeded in so thoroughly indoctrinating him that through his long life as an individual soul, man has fondly clung to the false idea of his separate existence. All his thoughts, ideas, emotions, experiences, and activities have always assumed, confirmed, and demonstrated to him the existence of the separate "I". To give up this deep-rooted belief—which he does not even suspect to be false—to yield what he believes to be the core of his identity, would mean surrendering all that seems to constitute his very existence. This is a prospect utterly beyond the capacity of the unenlightened even to contemplate, let alone accept.

To shed this last vestige of falsehood—to yield one's cherished identity—is therefore the most difficult of all tasks. Yet, in truth, this falsehood has no more substance than any of the earlier deceptions, which prior to awakening had seemed to the aspirant such unchallengeable certainties. Identification with the ego-mind too must eventually come to an end; it meets its doom when the soul renounces all craving for separate existence.

Countless are the falsehoods that Maya-ridden man, in the stupor of his ignorance, is duped into accepting; but from the very beginning all falsehoods carry within themselves the seeds of their own unmasking. Sooner or later in the evolutionary progress of the aspirant, their hollowness becomes evident and he recognizes them in their true colors, for the innate falsehoods they are. Even in the very depths of ignorance, at the inception of man's evolution, there is a faint stirring of challenge to the first falsehood that fastens itself upon the soul. However feeble and inarticulate this slender beginning of a protest, it is the dawn of that quest for the final truth that will ultimately lead to the annihilation of all ignorance, all falsehood. The usurpation of every subsequent falsehood is accompanied by a spontaneous though slow growth of inner restless-ness—a slight tremor of suspicion, a vague quiver of fear—born of the divine ferment implanted in the depth of the soul for its ultimate salvation.

Identification with the body, for example, brings with it the fear of one's own death and the fear of losing others. And in the very profundity of this fear—in man's heart of hearts—is seeded the first little sapling of suspicion that depending merely upon the possession of perishable forms for abiding happiness is building castles of hope on shadows of sand.

This is true of reliance on earthly possessions for security, and of all the other false premises with which Maya so enticingly paves the road of deception on which it diabolically leads man to his undoing. By the grace of God, however, there is a hollow sound to every flagstone of falsehood over which man is lured to walk toward his doom. The false note in the very sound, the sense of walking on thin ice camouflaged as pavement, betrays the fancy trappings of Maya to the growing spiritual intuition of the victim and eventually leads him to full consciousness of the Truth.

To achieve this, however, the aspirant must retrace his steps over the treacherous road he has traveled, and this is a task fraught with the most acute dangers. For not only is the surface flimsy and slippery, but Maya has cunningly changed the camouflage and shifted the landmarks, so that the victim now finds himself tragically lost in the labyrinth of a wilderness.

Frantically now he tries to escape, and in his anxiety is again and again fooled into following the innumerable false Maya lights that beckon him to bogus safety. Maya's task now is to conceal from the aspirant the one and only path that leads to his redemption. There is but one effective counterforce that can thwart the design of Maya and guide the aspirant to divine safety: the grace of the Perfect Master, who alone knows all the tricks of Maya and who alone on this earth is impervious to its wiles.

Through the grace of the Master the aspirant is enabled to distinguish the one true light from the myriad false ones, and to find his way out of the karmic wilderness into the eternal stronghold of God's Truth, which is impregnable to the assaults of Maya.

Not until then does the soul become lucidly aware of the all-absorbing truth that in the divine fact of Reality, Maya and the whole universe of deception created by it do not exist. Not until then does the soul know itself to be what it has always been: eternally self-realized; eternally infinite in all-knowledge, all-bliss, all-power, and all-existence; eternally free from duality; eternally, inseparably all-one in God.

THE RULE AND OVERTHROW OF THE EGO

THE FORMATION OF THE EGO SERVES THE PURPOSE of giving a certain measure of stability to conscious processes; it also provides a working equilibrium that makes for a planned and organized life. It would, therefore, be a mistake to assume that the rise of the ego is without a creative purpose. Though it emerges only to vanish in the end, the ego does fulfill a temporary need that cannot be ignored in the long journey of the soul.

The ego thus has a destined place and performs a specific mission in the evolution of consciousness. However, since the ego is the master agent of Maya, ingrained in its very nature is the ambition to transgress the boundaries of its ordained domain and to assume dictatorial powers over the soul. The most cunning weapon of the ego in achieving this is its fostering of a sense of separateness from the rest of creation; emphasis on difference from other forms of life and provocation of conflict with them are its favorite ammunition. Moreover, to conceal its identity and design, the ego masquerades under the false conceit of identification with the body. As long as its sly disguise remains undetected, it is the source of all the illusion that vitiates experience.

Unsurpassed in subtlety and deception, ruthless in tactics, the ego proceeds to consolidate its position by fair means or foul. The chief aim of its strategy is to deep-root and perennialize the sense of individual separateness, for the ego can best thrive in the jungle growth of spiritual ignorance thus fecundated in the mind of man. The ego is acutely aware that the sprouting of the first shoots of spiritual curiosity marks the beginning of its own doom. All its crafty maneuvering is consequently centered on one plot: to thwart or at least postpone indefinitely the germination of hyperphysical inquisitiveness. Inevitably, then, the ego becomes the chief hindrance to the enlightenment of consciousness, the most formidable foe of spiritual emancipation.

The dangers inherent in the growth of the ego are intensified by the fact that man is conscious of only a small surface fragment of the ego, unaware of the deeper might of its being, in which its real strength lurks. The ego is like an iceberg that shows only about one-eighth of its menacing bulk, which is submerged and out of sight. Likewise, only a fraction of the real ego becomes manifest in consciousness in the form of the individual "I"; the true immensity of the ego remains concealed in the dark and treacherous catacombs of the subconscious mind.

The ego feeds and grows fat on desires; the very act of desiring— regardless of results—is its meat. Success in the attainment of a coveted object is the triumph of the ego; failure to satisfy a craving is the ego's frustration. Both the gratification of desires and the inability to attain them contribute to the intensification of the ego. If it is subjected to curtailment in one direction, it seeks and forces compensating expansion in another. So determined is the ego to hold sway that if it fails to prevent the birth of awakening and finds itself overwhelmed by a flood of spiritual resolutions and endeavors, it changes disguise with Machiavellian skill and tries to save itself by fastening upon the very force that had been brought into play for the overthrow of its reign. Still more, the ego has the adaptability to feed even upon the periodical lulls in the surge of cravings.

The only experience that contributes to the deflation of the ego is the manifestation of pure love; the only aspiration that tends to dissipate the false sense of separateness is the unalloyed longing to become one with the Beloved. Craving, hatred, anger, fear, and jealousy are all *exclusive* attitudes that create and widen the gulf between oneself and the rest of life. Love alone is the *inclusive* approach that helps bridge this artificial, ego-created gap and break through the barrier of separation erected by false imagination.

The divine lover, too, longs, but he is free of craving. He hungers for union with the Beloved, and in seeking it, he finds his sense of the ego-centric "I" becoming less and less assertive. In love, the "I" does not think about self-preservation, just as the moth does not fear getting burned in the flame. Whereas the ego is the unflagging assertion of separateness, love is the joyous affirmation of oneness. Only true love can overcome the ego; only union with the Beloved can completely dissolve it.

In the ripeness of evolution, man at last arrives at the momentous discovery that life cannot be understood or lived fully so long as it is made to revolve around the false pivot of the ego. It is then that the inescapable logic of man's own experience impels him to seek the real center of his being—the spiritual sun of Truth—and to reorbit his life around it. This spiritual revolution necessitates the dethronement of the ego and its replacement by Truth-consciousness. Such an uprising against its dictatorship will inevitably be fought by the ego with all the formidable and sinister weapons at its disposal. In the process, man will discover that his liberation from the overlordship of the ego is in fact not possible without its complete annihilation; for as long as there is even the feeblest breath of life left in the hydra-headed ego, it has the toughness to resuscitate itself and the resources to reestablish its hegemony. Complete dissolution, therefore, of the false nucleus of accumulated and consolidated karmic impressions and tendencies—which is the mainspring of the ego's power—is an inescapable prerequisite to realization of the divine truth. The only road to true integration and fulfillment of life is over the dead body of the ego.

The consummation of this goal is the one all-vital task of every human being—an undertaking that few have the wisdom and courage, the strength and capacity, the tenacity and endurance, to successfully accomplish by themselves. It is the divine mission of the Perfect Master to light the path for the aspirant, to help him over the critical spots and guide him to his goal.

The ego is too deeply entrenched, its reserves too shrewdly deployed, its decoys too ingeniously concealed, for a successful frontal assault. The main strength of the ego must first be sapped; its shock troops—the elite corps of cravings—confounded and disorganized; its whole strategy foiled by a war of attrition. The most effective means of accomplishing this is not by attack, but by the subtle generalship of strategic withdrawal—withdrawal from desires. In no other way can the mighty forces of the ego be split up into harassed fragments, its cunningly mined fields avoided, its adroitly laid traps bypassed. Thus only can the impregnable might of the ego be made vulnerable, its scattered battalions lured into pockets of undoing, its triumphant forces reduced to impotence. Only by such a master stroke can the unbeatable armies of the ego be ultimately annihilated.

On the propaganda front, too, the utmost skill is necessary to counteract and neutralize the wily intrigue and subversive stealth of the ego. So clever is the disguise of its fifth-columnists of pride, vanity, prejudice, intolerance, conceit, holier-than-thou piety, ambition, smugness, and of its many other well-groomed secret agents, that they are not only practically unrecognizable as enemies, but even held close to the bosom as friends. The only thing that will smoke them out is recognition that the task entrusted to them by the ego is to implant in the mind and nurse into action the insidious doctrine of division and separateness from other creatures; the only countermeasure that will rout these satellite-termites of the ego is the deliberate, consistent assertion of unity, the daily living demonstration of oneness with all living beings.

Simultaneously with parallel master strategy on the battle and propaganda fronts against the ego, the home front, too, requires the most skillful statesmanship if the campaign against the hordes of the ego is to succeed. Here the deeper aspects of the conflict come into play.

One of the chief and most insidiously subversive fallacies on the home front is the ego-planted concept of "good" and "evil." It is the ego's job to conjure up a false standard of "right" and "wrong" for man, and to mislead him into gauging his life and the life of others by it.

The ego has led man to believe that all he has to do for his salvation is to stop being "bad" and become "good." This is one of the ego's most pernicious snares. Next to the complexes of superiority and inferiority, it keeps more souls from liberation than any other device of the ego.

Apart from the fact that by design of the ego, standards of "good" and "bad" vary with the exigencies of time, clime, and nationality, one of the chief reasons why this false concept is so destructive is that it frequently results in an attitude of "holier-than-thou"— the perfect trap for the unwary. Granted, from the very beginning of human evolution, the process of emancipation consists in cultivating and developing higher karmic tendencies and deeds, so that they might overlap and eventually annul the accumulated lower ones. Two cardinal facts, however, the ego deliberately keeps from its victims.

One of these all-vital facts is that whether a person happens to be "good" or "bad" at any given time depends upon the inexorable operation of his karmic ties. In the light of this ultimate standard, saint and sinner are both what they are because of the immutable laws operative in the universe. Both have the same beginning, and the same end. From the divine point of view, and contrary to existing religions and creeds—so craftily instigated and popularized by the ego—no sinner carries the eternal stigma of degradation, no saint the eternal distinction of honor. No saint, however godlike, has attained the heights of moral excellence without having had many lives of moral failing; no sinner is so debased that he will not eventually rise from his ashes and ultimately achieve sainthood.

There is eternal, divine certainty of hope for everyone, without exception. None is utterly lost; none need ever despair. It remains true, however, that the way to divinity lies through renunciation of the base in favor of the noble.

The other unchangeable spiritual law that the ego takes such pains to hide from man is the target of a still more subtle strategy of distortion. The ego has no contrivance more effective in crippling the home front of man's crusade for self-liberation. The truth it so craftily conceals is that "good" deeds and experiences are also products of desire, and are therefore karmically no less binding than "bad" ones. Spiritual emancipation is possible only when "good" and "bad" balance each other, merging so completely in absolute neutralization of fulfillment that they leave no room for any further choice of self-desire.

The gradual unfoldment of "good" brings in its train love, generosity, and peace. The favorable karmic credits deposited by the manifestation of these qualities counterbalance and often overlap the debts of lust, greed, and anger. When the two sides are perfectly balanced, there is an instantaneous termination of both karmic debts and credits, and a simultaneous transition of consciousness from a state of bondage to a state of freedom. But what the ego is so particularly shrewd in suppressing is that both the credit and debit sides of the book of karma have to sum up to absolute equality before the karmic account of the aspirant can be closed. For the ego is fully aware that if it permits the aspirant to draw the final line beneath his two equally balanced karmic columns, this line becomes at once a mortal dagger through its own heart.

Because of this certainty the ego does its best to keep the aspirant's karmic account in a constant state of unbalance. And one of its cleverest frauds is to keep the account running by a surplus on the credit side of the ledger. For it is sly enough to know that the deepest instinct of man is for the "good," and all that remains for the ego to do is to hitch the horse of this true instinct to the false wagon of self-righteousness, and it has the aspirant licked. In the majority of cases the aspirant stays licked, because he is unaware that emancipation is not a matter of mere accumulation of virtue; it requires the most delicate troy-weight balancing of the evolutionary ledger. This is not a mathematical problem of matching what appear to be equal amounts on the two sides of the ledger, nor is it an automatic process that could be left to itself; rather it is one that requires the wisest, most painstaking, most exacting effort on the part of the aspirant.

Until man learns this — and it generally takes him many incarnations of triumph and frustration to learn it — he falls again and again for the honeyed words of his ego, the tempter that ever builds new false mansions for him to dwell in, abodes to suit and perpetuate the particular Maya-distorted consciousness of the individual. Frequently this is a fool's paradise in the happy valley of self-deception, in which dwell people who are tricked by the ego into believing that salvation is achieved by *denial* of the existence of "evil."

In this valley of spiritual monomania dwell also the gullible who are roped into believing that the road to salvation lies by way of *affirmation*. The ego has convinced these poor deluded, whose number is growing into legion, that they can get anything they want, when they want it, including redemption, by riding roughshod over everything, even God, if necessary.

Between these extremes are people of many other, less assertive categories: honest, well-meaning, good, and kindly people. All are led by the ego on puppet strings away from the divine goal, under the delusion that "good" deeds, thoughts, and behavior alone assure salvation.

For those whom it cannot lure into this phantom land of spiritual mesmerism, the ego builds palaces of sanctimoniousness and self-worship. These imposing castles of the mind, too, are founded on ignorance and falsehood. The intoxicant that the ego uses on the unfortunate dwellers in these fancy self-prisons is the conviction that they need not strive for salvation; they have already achieved it. They need not aspire for heaven, since they have turned earth into heaven for themselves, even if they had to do so at the expense of turning it into hell for others.

All these "good" edifices are more difficult to dismantle than the "bad" ones that they supplant, because self-identification with the "good" becomes more easily deep-rooted than self-identification with the "bad." Inevitable pangs of conscience usually help man to recognize what is "bad" and assist him in ridding himself of it; but the "good" is generally robed in the garment of self-esteem and becomes a burr of righteousness that bores its way ever deeper into man's consciousness, until it becomes well nigh impossible to get rid of it.

The difficulty with the abode of "evil" lies not so much in perceiving it as a limitation as in dismantling it; the problem of the palace of "good" lies not so much in dismantling it as in perceiving it as a limitation. Both bind man alike. Their stranglehold is a problem of qualitative balancing. When this balancing is accomplished, both "good" and "evil" disappear, leaving a clean state of mind on which nothing is written and which therefore reflects the undistorted Truth. In this pure reflection the mind at last perceives the untarnished soul. This is *Illumination*. After the mind has beheld the soul, it must be merged in it before the soul can become conscious of itself. This is *Realization*. In this state the mind itself, with all its impressions and accumulations of "good" and "evil," and the ego-fostered perpetual strife between the two has disappeared. For the soul has at last come to dwell in a realm in which there is neither good nor evil, only God.

Another aspect of the home front where the subversive activities of the ego create confusion that is most disruptive to the aspirant's war of liberation is the sphere of superiority and inferiority complexes that motivate man's behavior and actions. These two destructive extremes have to be brought into delicately balanced polarity if they are to neutralize each other. And unless they are neutralized, the forces struggling against the hosts of the ego will be handicapped, if not brought to grief.

To achieve perfect counterpoise between these two basic, ego-planted tangles of the mind requires the creation of a psychic situation in which they are both induced, for a time, to come into full play simultaneously, without requiring the repression of the one in order to secure the expression of the other. It is only when the aspirant enters into dynamic, creative affinity with the Master that these two complexes are severed from the puppet strings of the ego and expend themselves in the impact of simultaneous demonstration of self-importance. The two complexes, which hold man in life-long thralldom, are thus brought into mutual tension by the attempt of the aspirant to enter into perfect kinship with the Master. Like two light rays of equal intensity, momentum, and quality, they annihilate each other at the point of equally balanced contact.

The dissolution of these opposite complexes automatically brings down with it the superstructure of separate barriers that the ego has so laboriously built up in consciousness, and of which they were the main pillars. The breaking down of the walls of separation opens the way for the influx of divine love. With the emergence of divine love as the dominant factor in the life of the aspirant, the false sense of isolation of the "I," as distinguished from the "you," dissolves into the greater consciousness of indivisible unity—an absolute essential for the triumph of the crusade against the ego.

In the course of his evolution, man has allowed himself to become too deeply entangled in the web woven about him by the assertive ego. Sapped of his divine creativeness by the age-old machinations of the ego, man has become incapable of successfully launching and victoriously consummating the Herculean campaign of annihilation against the all-powerful forces of the ego. Only the Perfect Master who functions on the ultimate plane of divine absoluteness has the all-knowing wisdom, the unhampered capacity, the indefatigable energy, and the inexhaustible endurance to marshal such a campaign and to guide it to victory.

To understand the function of the Perfect Master is to realize that he is the affirmation incarnate of the unity of all life. Unalloyed allegiance to him and implicit faith in his guidance open the way to the influx of the Master's love—the one solvent that not even the unparalleled toughness of the ego-nucleus can withstand. If, like a good soldier, the aspirant responds to the Master's command with unquestioned enthusiasm and carries his orders into execution with unqualified fervor, he will open the floodgates of his heart to the unimpeded influx of the Master's love. The irresistible potency of this divine solvent will finally disintegrate the ego and all the false concepts that are its offspring. In their place will flower the redeeming consciousness of divine oneness, of which the Master is the living embodiment.

When this greater awareness becomes the guiding incentive and vivifying principle in the life of the aspirant, it leads inevitably to his spiritual emancipation. For not only does it culminate in absolute union with the Master and, through the Master, with all creation, but in the supreme moment of merging with the Master in divine love, the aspirant attains the acme of his quest, which is the ultimate goal of all human beings: God-realization.

THE DYNAMICS
⌒ OF SPIRITUAL ADVANCEMENT ⌒

WORLDLY MAN lives mostly through and for the body. Even pursuits that seem to have little or no connection with the body, if traced to their source, will be found to have their roots in desires connected with the body. Man's spiritual advancement begins when he ceases catering to his body exclusively and transfers his chief attention to the requirements of the soul. This does not mean neglect of the body—on the contrary. From indulgence in abnormal appetites and gross physical habits, which tend to stimulate and excite the body rather than keep it in a healthy condition, man now reclaims his body for the purpose for which it was originally intended: to serve as the temple of the soul.

From the inception of spiritual awakening, man is no longer a slave to his body. Like the driver of a car who has a long distance to travel and keeps his motor well supplied with clean oil, good gasoline, and pure water—not to indulge his car but to ensure its perfect functioning— man now tends to the true needs of his body. He supplies it with wholesome, sensible food and guards it against contamination and abuse, only for the purpose of keeping it in perfect condition for the expression of the higher life. Instead of a hindrance, the body now becomes a help in the arduous task ahead.

Stirred by the incomprehensible and irresistible pull of his divine destiny, man proceeds to pursue his quest for spiritual emancipation. He soon discovers that the path is difficult, abounding with pitfalls and slippery precipices. Not infrequently he finds that after he had scaled great heights, the slightest mistake makes him lose his foothold and slide back, often plunging him to the bottom, where he has to start the precipitous climb all over again. And the journey is never the same, the path always new, changing even during the ascent, with every karmic change in the climber's fortunes. That is why the aspirant is never safe unless he has the help and guidance of a Perfect Master — the divine guide—who knows every inch of the treacherous path and how to lead the climber to the top without mishap.

The aspirant who has started on the spiritual path carries with him a vast accumulation of karmic impressions, tendencies, debts, and obligations. In the intensity of his spiritual longing they remain partially suspended and for a time inoperative, but time and again, with the slightest slackening of spiritual effort, this temporarily suspended mass of karmic debris re-arrays and reasserts itself into formidable, often impassable obstacles in the path of the aspirant. The problem may be likened to the flow of a river whose powerful current carries along with it great quantities of eroded earth, trees, brush, and other waste that it has picked up at its source, from its banks, and from its bed. As long as this mass is disbursed and suspended in the water, it does not hinder the flow of the river, though at times it might slacken it. But where the current slows down or becomes sluggish, particularly as it approaches the mouth, this vast residue has a tendency to settle on the bottom of the river, forming huge islands and deltas that not only obstruct the flow of the river, but often divert it and even split it into smaller currents, weakening and at times completely dissipating the great force of the once mighty river. The path of spiritual advancement is, in like manner, often blocked by obstacles of its own accumulation. These can be removed only with the help of the Perfect Master.

The objective of spiritual advancement is not so much "works" as the achievement of a quality of life that is free from the stranglehold of the ego. If the aspirant has great worldly achievements to his credit, and claims them as his own, his ego fastens itself upon his conceit, which it had cunningly engendered in him in the first place, and from this vantage point is able to seriously impede his spiritual progress. That is why rituals and ceremonies, the thumbing of holy books, acts of charity and good works, methodical attendance at religious services, external renunciation, and penances, are absolutely futile when they are rooted—as most often they are—in ego-consciousness.

To avoid this fatal pitfall, the aspirant should free himself of the very consciousness of "I do this" and "This is mine." It does not mean that he should refrain from all activity through fear of strengthening his ego. On the contrary, he may have to adopt a life of increased activity in order to wear down the ego he has already developed. The aspirant is thus caught in a baffling dilemma: if he remains inactive, he does nothing toward breaking out of the prison of his ego-life; if he takes to a life of action, he risks being caught in the new traps planted by his ego with the help of these very acts.

There is a very effective method to deal with this serious problem: the aspirant must surrender his limited ego-life in favor of the unlimited egoless life represented by the Master. Complete self-surrender is difficult to achieve; yet the most essential condition of spiritual advancement is the diminishing of the ego to its minimum. The aspirant, however, has been so accustomed to deriving his zest in life from the stimulation of his limited ego that an immediate transition from a life of egoistic action to one free from the ego would leave him completely bereft of inspiration. It would relegate him to a state of negative passivity, where there would be no room, no opportunity, for the joy of expression, or where he would be compelled to seek expression through automatic activity, like that of a lifeless machine, totally barren of any sense of fulfillment. Such a sudden transition would therefore be fatal.

The solution is to create a provisional working ego entirely subservient to the Master. In centering his life, for a time, around this transitory alter-ego, the aspirant should adopt the following procedure: Before launching upon an activity, whether trivial or important, he should feel and believe that it is not he who is doing it, but the Master, who is getting it done through him. When the activity is completed, the aspirant should not tarry to claim credit for the deed or exult over it; he should free himself of the last vestige of identification with the action by transferring its laurels to the Master. This procedure, if persisted in, creates for the aspirant a new ego, which though provisional and seemingly outside himself, has the capacity to become a source of that confidence, inspiration, enthusiasm, and "go" that motivate all spontaneous human action. But this new ego is spiritually harmless, since it derives its existence and functioning from the Master, who is the embodiment of ego-free Infinity and is therefore divinely immune to the sinister encroachment of the ego. When the time is ready, this provisional ego of the aspirant can be thrown away like a garment.

The creation of a new ego that is entirely subservient to the Master is indispensable in the dynamics of spiritual advancement.

EVOLUTION
∽ THROUGH THE THREE WORLDS ∼

WHILE DEVELOPING FULL CONSCIOUSNESS of the gross world in the human form, the soul simultaneously develops the subtle and mental bodies. As long as its sole awareness is confined to the gross world, however, the soul cannot use these bodies knowingly in wakefulness. It becomes cognizant of them and of the corresponding worlds only when its full consciousness is turned inward, toward itself. When the soul becomes aware of the subtle world through the subtle body, it identifies itself with the subtle body, and when it becomes conscious of the mental world through the mental body, it assumes identity with the mental body, in the same way that it identified itself with the gross body when consciousness of the gross world came to it through that body. The homeward journey of the soul consists in freeing itself from the illusory identity with all of its bodies—gross, subtle, and mental.

The soul is, always has been, and ever will be inseparably one with the Oversoul. In the primal beginning, however, it had no developed consciousness and was therefore unaware of its identity with the Oversoul. Throughout the first stages of evolving consciousness, the soul is still unaware of its oneness with the Oversoul; its consciousness is confined to the various aspects of the phenomenal world, owing to the karmic impressions, tendencies, and obligations that limit its growth. Even after the aspirant has entered the spiritual path, the soul does not yet become conscious of its true identity; its awareness extends only to the gross, subtle, and mental worlds, which are its own illusory shadows.

When the aspirant reaches the end of his quest, his soul has become free of all the karmic desires and limitations connected with the gross, subtle, and mental worlds. Liberated from the falsehood of the past, the soul is now able to extricate itself from the illusion of finitehood, which owes its existence to the soul's identification with the gross, subtle, and mental bodies. In this ultimate moment of redemption, the soul completely transcends the phenomenal world and becomes self-conscious, and self-realized. To attain this goal, the soul must retain full consciousness and at the same time know itself to be wholly independent of the gross, subtle, and mental bodies. It must be aware that the gross, subtle, and mental worlds are products of illusion, and become divinely conscious of its own transcendental supremacy over them.

∼ EVOLUTION THROUGH THE OPPOSITES ∼

THE MENTAL AND EMOTIONAL TENDENCIES accumulated by specific actions and experiences in the past render the ego-mind susceptible to similar actions and experiences in the present and in the future. After a certain point of saturation is reached, however, this tendency is checked and counterbalanced by a natural reaction that manifests in a complete shift toward the opposite direction. Its aim is to clear the way for the operation of reverse tendencies.

This phenomenon occurs when the ego discovers the incompleteness of its share of an experience and instinctively seeks to restore the lost balance by going over to its opposite. Thus, one who has had the experience of killing will develop the psychic need to get killed, and the susceptibility to it. The act of killing brings to the aggressor only one part of the complete experience: that of killing. The other half of the total act, the complementary role of being killed, remains for him an unknown and unexplored aspect, which nevertheless becomes in the act an inseparable though unfulfilled part of his karma. From this moment, the slayer becomes subject to karmic determinism, which compels completion of the cycle, and encourages it by attracting to the aggressor factors essential to the rounding out of the experience. The destiny of the killer is not fulfilled until he has actually gone through the personal ordeal of being at the receiving end of murder.

Like the shuttle of the weaver's loom, the human mind is compelled to move between fateful opposites, developing the warp and woof of the cloth of life. The evolution of the psychic life is best represented not as a straight line but as a zigzag course. The oscillation becomes less and less as one approaches the ultimate goal, and subsides completely with its attainment.

KARMIC IMPRESSIONS AND TENDENCIES (SANSKARAS)

THE ACQUISITION OF EVOLUTIONARY IMPRESSIONS, tendencies, and emotions may be likened to the incessant winding of an endless string around an inert ball, the string representing the impressions, tendencies, and emotions, and the ball the mind of the individual soul. This winding process starts at the very beginning of creation and persists through all the evolutionary stages, including the human cycle. The string symbolizes all the mind's impressions—natural as well as nonnatural—and all the mental and emotional tendencies accumulated in the course of evolution.

Human beings fail in self-illumination because their consciousness is entwined in these impressions and veiled by the maze of accumulated imprints of past experiences. The will-to-be-conscious, which sprang into spontaneous being simultaneously with the birth of the first phenomenon in the cycle of evolution, comes to fruition in the form of human consciousness. It is, however, thwarted in its effort to arrive at the ultimate destination of its quest—awareness of the Oversoul—because the ego-mind is too deeply engrossed in accumulating and acting upon its karmic impressions, and counterbalancing the avalanche of tendencies created by them. Individual consciousness is expended in this all-absorbing process; it does not have sufficient momentum left for the cardinal task of experiencing its own true nature as the Oversoul.

Only when consciousness is freed from its impediments and purged of its accumulated impressions and tendencies does the initial will-to-be-conscious arrive at its final and true destination: conscious realization of the infinity and indivisible unity of the Absolute. In the search for ultimate truth, it is therefore of prime essence that man first obtain release from the karmic bondage of the past. There are five different ways in which this may be accomplished:

1. *The cessation of new impressions.*
This consists in putting an end to the ceaseless activity of creating fresh impressions and tendencies. If the formation of mental impressions is compared to the winding of a string around a ball, this step is equivalent to putting a stop to the winding of any further string.

2. *The wearing out of old impressions.*
If accumulated impressions and tendencies are deliberately withheld from expressing themselves in action and experience, they gradually wear out. In our analogy, this process is comparable to the disintegration of the string through lack of use.

3. *The unwinding of past impressions.*
This is achieved by the annulment of past impressions through mentally reversing the processes that originally led to their formation. Repentance, augmented by profound self-condemnation, is the procedure, and it may be compared to the freeing of the ball by unwinding the string.

4. *The dispersion and exhaustion of impressions.*
If the psychic energy that is imprisoned in the karmic impressions and tendencies is sublimated and diverted into other channels, they are exhausted in the effort, become dispersed, and tend to disappear. The ball, no longer inert, bursts its binding strings.

5. *The wiping out of impressions.*
This consists of completely annihilating past impressions and their resultant tendencies, a process comparable to cutting the string into shreds, thereby liberating the ball. The final wiping out of accumulated karmic impressions and tendencies can be effected only by the grace of a Perfect Master.

⌒ REINCARNATION AND KARMA ⌒

THE OVERWHELMING IMPORTANCE man attaches to death is the result of his attachment to outer forms. Age-old superstition, inculcated in his mind by orthodox creeds, makes it difficult, if not impossible, for the average man to accept reincarnation as a fact. Reincarnation has been an immutable, divine fact from the first manifestation of creation; it is so now and will continue to be, regardless of whether man, in his unawareness, refuses to accept it as a fact. In the course of spiritual evolution, all human beings reach a point of consciousness when the fact of reincarnation becomes vividly clear to them; and when it does, the phenomenon of death assumes an entirely new aspect: it reveals the innate beauty and sublimity of its creative place in the divine pattern of life.

Even for the worldly man, death can lose much of its sting when he acquires the wisdom to take a broader view of life. Regardless of the finite limitations of the intellect, he can accept it as a postulate that in spite of the transitoriness of visible forms — in fact, in and through these forms — there is an unbroken continuity of life, which discards old forms and forges new ones for its habitation and manifestation. The recurring incident of death is balanced by the recurring incident of birth. In spite of the unceasing activity of the hand of death, life continues to flourish. Old generations are replaced by new ones, and life reappears in fresh garments, incessantly renewing and refreshing itself. The stream of life throughout eternity is forever advancing through constantly changing forms, which come and go like the waves of the ocean.

Hell and heaven are states of the mind; they should not be regarded as actual locales. Although, from the subjective point of view, belief in these concepts exerts a powerful influence on the individual, they are both illusions within the greater illusion of the phenomenal world.

The experiences of earthly life, as well as the processes of reflection and integration through which the soul passes in life after death, are merely contributories to the main stream of intuitive wisdom, which is already latent in the soul from the very beginning of creation, and which reaches the full majesty of its flow at the moment of spiritual realization.

Except in rare instances, knowledge about past lives is not necessary for charting the onward course of spiritual evolution. Inner progression consists in guiding the life of the present in the light of the highest precepts perceived through the intuition, and not in subjecting it to the dominance of the past.

Though the opportunities afforded with each incarnation vary with time, place, sex, age, and environment, each incarnation is predestined and affords special facilities for the unfolding of experiences along specific lines. The lessons that are readily learned in male incarnations may not be easily absorbed through female incarnations; and the reverse too is true. Men, as a rule, excel in the qualities of head and will; they are capable of sound judgment and steadfast purpose. Women generally shine in the qualities of the heart; they are capable of intense love, which conditions them to welcome any sacrifice for the loved one.

The soul must go through both male and female incarnations if it is to acquire the richness of experience that is prerequisite to realizing that the soul is beyond all forms of duality, including the overemphasized duality of sex.

The problem of sexual duality is part of the intrinsic problem of the whole of duality; it is automatically solved with the overall solution of duality itself through divine love, in which there is neither "I" nor "you," neither man nor woman.

In the world of physical phenomena, the law of conservation of energy, according to which no energy is ever lost, is an accepted fact. In the realm of spiritual values, too, it is an unalterable law that once karma—the principle of evolutionary cause and effect—comes into existence in the life of an individual, it does not mysteriously disappear without fulfilling its natural function. It persists until it bears its own fruit or is undone by counterkarma. Consequently, it is karmically inevitable for "good" deeds to lead to good results and "bad" actions to bad consequences.

If a person has done an evil turn to someone, he is fated to receive the penalty for it and must welcome the evil thus brought upon himself in the knowledge that it is a debt paid. If he has done a good turn to a fellow human being, it is his destiny to receive a reward for it, and he must enjoy the good that comes to him, in the realization that it too is a debt discharged. What he does to another, he has also done to himself, although it may take time for him to realize how true this is. The law of karma might be said to be the working of divine justice—a demonstration of the inseparable, timeless unity of all life, beneath the transitory surface of the world of duality.

⌒ LUST, GREED, AND LOVE ⌒

INFATUATION, LUST, AND GREED may be regarded as lower, perverted forms of love. In infatuation, man becomes enamored of a desirable creature; in lust, he develops sensual appetite for it; in greed, he craves to possess it. Blind, passive surrender to the spell of carnal attraction is the bane of infatuation; active, aware appreciation of the intrinsic worth of the beloved is the blessing of love.

Lust is the lowest, most distorted form of love. In lust, sole reliance is upon the quarry of the senses, with consequent spiritual subordination of the soul: the sensualist is virtually anchored to the prey of his lust. Love, however, puts the soul in direct and reciprocal touch with the Reality that is behind and beyond the form. Lust, therefore, may be called an experience heavy with the weight of its own corruption, while the exaltation of love seems to lend wings to the participants. In lust, there is a dwarfing of life; in love, an expansion of being. The sterility of lust depletes the spirit; it generates a sense of hopeless dependence upon a form that is regarded as belonging to another entity. Love enhances the spirit; its sacred fire fuses the lives of lover and beloved into one, doubling the capacity of both. Loving the whole world is, in the deepest sense, equivalent to living in the whole world. Lust is a blundering into separateness and grief; love, a progression into unity and joy. Lust is dissipation; love, regeneration. Lust is the craving of the senses; love, the reaching out of the spirit. In lust, there is excitement; in love, tranquillity. Lust seeks fulfillment; love experiences it.

Greed, too, has little in common with love. Greed is possessive in all its gross and subtle forms. It covets and appropriates coarse objects and people, as well as such ephemeral things as money, power, and fame. Love seeks and attracts things and persons of beauty, and values of lasting significance. The very idea of exclusive possession is unthinkable in love. There is, in love, a lavish creative outpouring of the spirit that quickens and replenishes the psychic being of the beloved; it is wholly free from any expectations for itself. Greed, which drives the self to appropriate the target of its craving, ends in slavery to it; love, whose spontaneous joy it is to give away the self to the object of its longing, leads in fact to absorption of the beloved in the very being of the lover. In greed, the self tries to possess the object but is itself spiritually possessed by it; love lays the self at the feet of the beloved without any reservations, yet in that very act it finds the beloved becoming a spiritual part of its own being.

In the fulfillment of love, reason plays a part. The interrelationship between the two is of three kinds. In the first, the sphere of love and the sphere of thought are kept as separate as possible; here the domain of love is practically closed to the expression of reason, while love is allowed little or no access to the realm of thought. Complete separation between these two expressions of the spirit is, of course, never possible, but where there is alternate functioning of love and reason—an oscillation of predominance—we have a love unillumined by reason and a reason unsweetened by love.

In the second type, love and reason are operating simultaneously, but they do not work in harmony with each other. Though this conflict creates confusion, it is a necessary phase in the evolution toward the highest state, where there is true synthesis of love and reason.

This ideal blending of love and reason becomes an accomplished fact in the third kind of interrelation between the two. In this highest manifest-ation of their respective functions, both love and reason are completely transformed; they emerge as one on a new level of awareness—beyond what is known as normal—into a state that may best be described as superconsciousness.

It is due to love that contact and communion between human beings assume significance; it is love that invests with meaning and value all that happens in the world of duality. But while love gives meaning to the world of duality, it is at the same time a standing challenge to it. As love gathers strength, it generates creative restlessness and becomes the main driving force of that spiritual dynamic that ultimately succeeds in restoring to consciousness the original unity of being.

The pure, wholly selfless love that is awakened through the grace of the Master is of greater spiritual value in the life of the aspirant than any other means that he may adopt in search of the Truth. Such love not only combines within itself the merits of all spiritual disciplines, but excels them all in the technique of leading the aspirant to his goal. When such a love comes to the aspirant, he has but one desire: to be united with the Divine Beloved. Such withdrawal of consciousness from all other desires leads to infinite virtue; nothing purifies one more completely than such a love for the Master. It inspires the aspirant to offer his all to the Divine Beloved. No sacrifice is too difficult for him; all his thoughts are withdrawn from the self and come to be centered exclusively in the Divine Beloved. Through the ever-growing intensity of this love, the aspirant eventually breaks the shackles of the self and becomes united with the Beloved. This is the consummation of true love; for in the ultimate flowering of its God-essence in the Master, the love of the aspirant achieves divinity.

Divine love is in all aspects different from human love. Human love is for the many in the one; divine love is for the one in the many. Human love creates innumerable complications and entanglements; divine love leads to integration and freedom. In human love, the duality of the lover and the beloved persists; in divine love, the lover and the Beloved become one. At this stage, the aspirant has transcended the domain of duality and become one with God; for divine love is God. In the supreme moment when lover and Beloved become one, the end of the quest is merged with the beginning of bliss.

The whole universe sprang into being for the sake of divine love; out of love was it created, because of it, it endures, through it will it regain its source. Man's supreme goal is to transmute the timeless love-urge within him into the God-essence of divine love. The merging of the two will dissolve all iniquity; it will give birth to what has so long been spoken of as the kingdom of heaven on earth.

⌒ SEX, MARRIAGE, AND CELIBACY ⌒

PROMISCUITY IN SEXUAL GRATIFICATION is bound to land the aspirant in the most pitiful and dangerous chaos of ungovernable lust. In promiscuousness the suggestions of lust are inevitably the first to present themselves to the mind. This dooms the sensualist to react every time within the gross pattern of the initial perversion, and with each indulgence to seal tighter the door to nobler experiences.

Among the chief characteristics of promiscuity is a growing sense of frustration and disappointment. When this becomes too acute, the mind resorts to forced, external repression of cravings. This inevitably results in further intensification of sex-hunger and often in sexual abnormalities. But when disappointment makes way for disillusionment or true awakening, the mind yields to the higher instinct of spontaneous inner renunciation. One phase of this is celibacy.

The value of celibacy lies in the habit of restraint and in the sense of detachment and independence that are its fruits. But as long as the mind is not completely free from craving, it cannot know true freedom. The value of marriage, on the other hand, is to be found in the lessons of mutual adjustment and the sense of unity between man and woman that characterize true wedlock. Absolute union, however — complete annihilation of duality — is possible only through divine love, which can never nest in the heart so long as there is the slightest shadow of lust or craving in the mind. Only by treading the path of spontaneous inner renunciation of craving is it possible to attain true freedom and unity. This path of spiritual perfection is open to the aspirant whether in celibacy or marriage. Which of these he chooses will depend upon his karmic impressions, tendencies, and ties.

Sex in true matrimony is entirely different from sex outside matrimony. In marriage, the tendencies of lust are much weaker and consequently more readily removed. When sexual companionship in marriage is ennobled by love, illumined by spiritual idealism, and enhanced by a sense of responsibility, conditions for the sublimation of sex are much more favorable than in an atmosphere of promiscuousness.

In marriage, the range of mutual experiences is so wide that suggestions of lust are not necessarily the first to present themselves; this gives the aspirant a real opportunity to recognize and counteract the limiting factors in his path. By the gradual elimination of lust, and the substitution of increasingly richer marital experiences of selfless love and sacrifice, the aspirant can finally arrive at Infinity.

The spiritual value of married life is in direct ratio to the nature of the dominant factors that characterize its daily routine. In the beginning the partners are generally drawn to each other by lust as well as love; but they can, through conscious and deliberate cooperative effort, gradually lessen the intrusion of lust and increase the element of love. Through this process of sublimation, lust ultimately disintegrates and gives way to pure love. Through the heartfelt sharing of joys and sorrows, and through conscious ascendancy over gross instincts, the partners can progress from one spiritual triumph to another, from deep love to ever-deeper love, until the possessive and jealous relationship of the initial period is entirely replaced by a love of selflessness and self-giving. When matrimony is thus brought into direct line with the divine plan for the evolution of the individual, it becomes a pure blessing to the children who are the fruit of such a union, for they have the priceless advantage of imbibing the ennobling vibrations of a spiritual atmosphere from the very beginning of their earthly careers.

In true marriage there is no place for birth control as practiced by the misguided masses. From the spiritual point of view, birth control must essentially be effected by mental restriction and in no other way. Mental power is necessarily undermined by reliance on physical means. The use of such means is detrimental to the development of self-control and most disastrous to spiritual advancement. Physical means of birth control are therefore under no condition advisable, however lofty the motives; they inevitably intensify the element of lust and lower the level of married life.

If matrimony is based upon shallow considerations, it can easily deteriorate into a partnership of selfishness against the rest of the world. If, however, it is inspired by true devotion and consecrated by exalted idealism, it can rise to a fellowship that calls forth increasingly greater mutual sacrifices, and results in ever-mounting experiences of spiritual growth. Thus purified, marriage has the potentiality to become a medium through which the pure love and selfless service of the two united souls can achieve a momentum abundant enough to enrich the whole family of mankind.

⌒ SELFLESS SERVICE ⌒

SELFLESS SERVICE is unaffected by results. It is like the rays of the sun that serve the world by shining alike on all creation: on the grass in the field, on the birds in the air, on the beasts in the forest, on all mankind; on saint and sinner, rich and poor, strong and weak—wholly impervious to their attitude or reaction.

It is of vital importance, however, that service, though utterly selfless, be guided by spiritual understanding; for even selfless service unintelligently handled often creates complications and chaos. To be a pure blessing to humanity, the most selfless act of service must be born of absolute understanding of life and governed by faultless wisdom.

Selfless service consists in rendering service to others with no thought of gain, reward, or result; it is free from the thought of placing others under obligation. In serving a fellow human being in the spirit of spontaneous, selfless love, one does not put him under obligation. On the contrary, the one helped confers upon the helper the blessing of an opportunity to serve his own true self.

There is complete disregard of one's own convenience or welfare in selfless service; it is characterized by absolute subjugation of one's own happiness—by unalloyed joy in sacrificing everything for the well-being of others. In selfless service the comfort of others is one's convenience, their health one's healing, their happiness one's delight. Giving one's life for others, one gains glorious life for oneself. Sheltering others in one's heart makes one inhabit theirs. An act of helpfulness, a word of comfort, the spontaneous warmth of selfless love, give to others what they greatly need. Their thoughts of gratitude and goodwill, the heightened surge of their spirit, and the increased flow of God-love released by the selfless act bring to the giver infinitely more than he can ever give.

Service performed after realization of the divine law of the universe is a spontaneous expression of spiritual understanding; it is rooted in full comprehension of the true nature of the self. Though it is followed by important results in the objective world, it is in no way affected or complicated by craving for such results. The sun shines because it is its nature to do so, not out of any ambition to achieve something by it; the God-realized person lives a life of spontaneous self-offering, prompted by the heart of the divine Reality with which he knows himself to be one, not out of longing to achieve anything for himself. The God-conscious do not seek enrichment through attainments, for having realized the Infinite, they are already established in the divine sufficiency of the universe.

Selfless service reaches its acme in the God-realized Master. The Perfect Master serves the whole universe out of the finality of his infinite consciousness; those who serve the Master or submit to his guidance share in his universal work. Their service has the advantage of the Master's wisdom and insight. Willing participation in the work of the Master not only enhances the value of the disciple's service, but also creates most favorable opportunities for spiritual enlightenment. In importance, service originating in the instructions of the Master is second only to the service rendered by the Master himself. Selfless service is a road that leads to God.

∽ UNIVERSAL SELFHOOD ∾

BEFORE DUALITY CAN BE COMPLETELY TRANSCENDED, selfishness must be transmuted into selflessness. This can be achieved by persistent and continuous performance of good deeds, which wears out selfishness. Channeled into good deeds, selfishness becomes the instrument of its own destruction. If persisted in, good deeds form a plank over which selfishness is made to walk to its doom.

Good deeds have a tendency to purify the doer. From good, the soul passes on to God. Selfishness becomes merged with Universal Selfhood, which is beyond good and bad, virtue and vice, and all the other dual aspects of illusion. From the peak of selflessness is perceived the vista of oneness with all creation. On this level there is neither selfishness nor selflessness in the ordinary sense; both are merged in and absorbed by a feeling of selfness for all. This exalted state of liberation brings about undisturbed harmony without loss of discrimination, unshakable peace without indifference to surroundings.

To reach this summit of realization, man must liberate his heart by weeding out all desires and by cultivating only one longing: the longing for union with God—the one ultimate Reality.

⌒ THE SEARCH FOR GOD ⌒

GOD EITHER EXISTS or does not exist. If He exists, search for Him is amply justified; and even if He does not exist, there is nothing to lose by seeking Him. However, man's search for God is usually not a voluntary and joyous enterprise. As a rule, he has to be driven to it by disillusionment over worldly things that allure him and to which his mind is slave.

When a man puts his heart into an intelligent and purposeful exploration of his own life, an increasingly deeper comprehension of the true meaning of all life comes to him, until finally he discovers that while undergoing complete transformation of his own psychic being, he has at the same time also achieved a clearer perception of the true significance of life itself. With this unclouded, mature vision of the ultimate nature and worth of life, the simultaneous realization comes to man that God, whom he has so desperately sought, is no stranger, no hidden or foreign entity. He becomes aware that God is Reality itself and not a mere hypothesis: the Reality that includes all and excludes nothing; the very Reality of which man himself is a part and in which he has his entire being; the God-Reality with which in fact man is identical.

Thus, although in his search for God man begins by seeking something apart from himself something utterly new, what he actually attains is a new understanding of the ancient truth. The spiritual journey does not consist in arriving at a new destination, gaining possession of something that man never had before; nor becoming something that he had never been. It consists in uprooting his ignorance concerning himself and life. Finding God is arriving at one's own self.

⌒ THE ONE AND THE MANY ⌒

THE ONE SUPREME BEING descends into the domain of illusion and seemingly assumes a multiplicity of forms and phenomena that do not in fact exist. In reality there is no separateness between individuals; it appears only in imagination. All human beings are, in the deepest sense, linked to all other human beings by divine tendons of spiritual oneness. The manifoldness apparent in the universe—the ostensible separateness between creature and creature, between one thing and another—is an entrancing phenomenon projected by the one supreme soul as an experiment in celestial fantasy. The effect, to the limited eye, is much the same as the illusory multiplication of one person or object by the countless reflections in a many-mirrored room. Out of this imaginary division arises in the mind of man the illusory concept of "I" and "mine" as opposed to "you" and "yours." Although the soul of the universe is in reality an absolute and undivided Unity, which includes and contains all there is, the myriad light-fragments of its own reflected imagination give the surface impression of division and manifoldness. This illusion—though seemingly as vividly real as a mirage—is no part of reality, and consequently all its products are illusory.

This becomes clear and subject to no intellectual doubt when one reaches the summit of Realization. From this vantage point one becomes aware that the Infinite is the one and only Reality; there is no one else, no other thing outside the Infinite, which permeates and includes all creation so absolutely that there is no room for any rival existence.

When man rises to recognition of this Oneness of all, he accomplishes the highest state of Realization. In this sphere he retains full evolutionary consciousness but is no longer bound by the limitations of illusion and desire. His limited individuality—a product of ignorance—is here transmuted into the divine individuality that knows no limitations. In this state, the illimitable consciousness of the universal soul becomes individuated without yielding its oneness, incarnate without giving rise to any form of illusion.

∽ THE SEVEN REALITIES ∽

THE ONLY REAL EXISTENCE IS THAT OF THE ONE AND ONLY GOD,
WHO IS THE SELF IN EVERY ONE.

The only real Love
is the love for God.

The only real Sacrifice
is that which knows no reservations.

The only real Renunciation
is the giving up of all selfish thoughts
and desires even in the midst of worldly duties.

The only real Knowledge
is the recognition that God is the inner dweller
in all—in good and bad—without exception.

The only real Self-Control
is complete mastery over gross desires.

The only real Surrender
is absolute yielding to the will of God.

ACTION AND INACTION

INACTION is in many ways preferable to unintelligent action, for it has at least the merit of not creating further karmic complications. Even good and righteous action sows the seeds of new complexities, which thicken the jungle that past actions and experiences have grown in the mind. All life is an effort to attain freedom from self-created entanglements, a desperate, ceaseless, though usually unconscious struggle to undo what had unwittingly been committed in the past, to discard the accumulated burden of our yesterdays, to get clear of the debris piled up by our temporal achievements and failures. The ultimate goal of life is to achieve unhampered freedom, to mature into that intrinsic richness of being that knows no limitations.

The progression from unwise action to enlightened action—from entangling experiences to redeeming experiences—is often through inaction. This transitory stage is characteristic of that moment in life when unintelligent action has stopped because of critical doubt, and intelligent action has not yet begun for want of adequate momentum. This passivity may be called creative inaction, which plays a useful part in man's spiritual progress. It should not be confused with the ordinary type of inaction, which is born of inertia or parented by fear of life.

~ MIND AND HEART ~

IN THE LIFE OF MOST PEOPLE, the mind and the heart are constantly at loggerheads, and the conflict between the two creates perpetual confusion. In its self-seeking manipulation of the material world, the mind becomes saturated with experiences of separateness and multiplicity. This feeds the egocentric tendencies that divide man from man and make him selfish and possessive. The heart, on the other hand, is quickened by the glow of love, which comes to it through its inner experiences, and by the glimpses of spiritual unity with which it is rewarded. It therefore seeks expression through self-giving tendencies, which unite man with man and make him selfless and generous.

When the mind encroaches upon the province of the heart, it requires the assurance of conviction before it will sanction the release of love. But love is nothing if not spontaneous. It is not born of reasoning, nor is it the fruit of bargaining. If man's mind insists on first being convinced or assured about the object of his longing before giving it his love, he is indulging in nothing more than a form of calculated selfishness.

The mind is the thesaurus of learning, the heart the treasure house of love and spiritual wisdom. Mind arrogates to itself the right to tell man what things are worth having, but it has neither the authority nor the capacity to do so. All it can do is indicate *how* to achieve ends inspired by promptings deeper than its own shallowness; it cannot originate them. In most people, the mind is a slave to wants and cravings by which they allow themselves to be driven. This results in the denial of the life of the spirit. The mind can enhance the life of the spirit only when its ideals and values are inspired by the deepest persuasions of the heart.

Spiritual understanding is born of harmony between mind and heart. Such harmony does not require interchange of effort, nor does it imply cross-function; it calls for cooperative functioning. The spheres of the mind and the heart are neither identical nor coordinate. True, the mind and the heart must be balanced, but this cannot be achieved by pitting the mind against the heart or the heart against the mind. It cannot be attained by physical tension, but only through intelligent adjustment. The mind and the heart are truly balanced when they serve their appointed purposes and perform their divinely allotted tasks in perfect rhythm with each other; only when they are thus poised can there be true harmony between them. Such intimate rapport between mind and heart is the most vital prerequisite of an integrated, balanced life of spiritual understanding.

⌒ THE PATH AND THE PLANES ⌒

TREADING THE SPIRITUAL PATH consists in neutralizing the results of the mental-emotional impressions and tendencies accumulated by karmic experiences. It entails the removal of the impenetrable veils that have created in the aspirant a sense of insurmountable separateness and irredeemable isolation.

Each definite stage of advancement represents a state of consciousness, and the advancement from one state of consciousness to another proceeds side by side with the progression from one inner plane to another. There are six intermediate planes and states of consciousness that have to be experienced before the attainment of the seventh plane—the end of the journey—which is simultaneous with the realization of the God-state. The inner planes are comparable to railway stations in which trains halt for a while; the states of consciousness may be likened to the movements of passengers when they alight at the stations.

When the aspirant enters a new inner plane, he becomes merged with it, and along with the lessening of illusive mental activity he experiences a substantial diminution of the ego-life. This curtailment of the ego-life is different in character from the final annihilation of the ego, which takes place on the seventh plane. In attaining this egoless state of ultimate consciousness, the pilgrim becomes permanently merged in God—and is, in fact, none other than God Himself.

∼OCCULTISM AND SPIRITUALITY ∼

WHILE THE ASPIRANT is experiencing psychic unfoldment, occasional manifestations of the subtle world will come to him in the form of significant visions, lights, colors, sounds, odors, bodiless journeys, and contacts. At first, these experiences are erratic and the aspirant is likely to treat them as hallucinations; yet however superficial his reaction, their intrinsic potency is so great that he will find it impossible to resist their influence. This is because they play an important part in the process of his spiritual illumination. These phenomena often bear unmistakable credentials of their claim to validity; but even where such proof is not self-evident, they compel attention and respect because of the unique significance and influence, peace and bliss, with which they are often endowed. These attributes, characteristic of genuine occult experiences, are good criteria by which to distinguish them from hallucinations and illusions.

Occult phenomena that are experienced by the aspirant involuntarily are of much less importance than those in which he participates in full consciousness and as a result of deliberate volition. The aspirant is therefore advised not to treat these experiences lightly or to dismiss them as of no significance. On the contrary, it will be of great assistance to him if he will give them his full-hearted interest and cooperation. Being merely the passive recipient of occult experiences results in slower progress for the aspirant than if he confines himself to putting into practice the noblest intuitions of his heart. Occult experiences are vouchsafed the aspirant only when absolutely necessary for his spiritual development, and not to satisfy his curiosity or in answer to his demand.

When occult experiences are the gift of the Master or of spiritually advanced souls, they serve the purpose of unveiling much of the hitherto obscured intuitions of the aspirant; they help to remove some of the difficulties in his path and are intended to impart to him an increasing sense of that confidence and enthusiasm which are so indispensable in coping with the new requirements of each stage of progress.

There are a number of outward actions characteristic of the relationship between Master and disciple that to the uninitiated may seem of little or merely archaic significance, but which have, in fact, profound occult meaning. Among these is the touching of the feet of a Perfect Master with one's hands and forehead, then touching one's forehead with the same fingers. With this deeply symbolic gesture, the disciple or pilgrim actually lays his karmic burden upon the Master, while the touching of the forehead signifies both that the devotee performs this action in full consciousness of its significance, and that in the act he surrenders his ego-mind, which stands in the way of his emancipation. The Master collects the karmic burden of the world, just as an ordinary person gathers upon his feet the dust of the road. And the Master, being above and beyond karma, can dispose of the burden, however vast, with the same ease with which the ordinary wanderer washes the dust of the road, however thick, off his feet.

Another procedure that belongs in this sphere has to do with removing the veil from the inner eye of the aspirant. When, with the help of the Master, the inner eye is opened, the disciple actually sees God, the age-old object of his search and longing. This is part of the helpful occult experiences the Master brings to the disciple to speed his regeneration. As the gaze of the soul is turned inward and fixed upon the heavenly beauty of the Supreme Reality, the longing and determination for union with it become infinitely more intense than in groping for an invisible God through mere speculation or imagination. When the time for the disciple is ripe, the Perfect Master can give sight to this inner eye in less than an instant.

The ultimate goal of the aspirant is to realize that God is the only Reality—that he himself is in profound fact one with God, and therefore one with divine Reality. To reach the pinnacle of this understanding, the disciple must first be freed from the hypnotic effect of the multiform world. He must come to know that the whole structure of the universe is in fact within his own self; that it springs into illusory existence from a minute point in the core of his being; that it shapes into apparent form out of the infinitesimal God-atom, which is immune to size, unencumbered by space, and free from the limitations of time.

The unveiling of the inner eye brings this impalpable point-sublime of the cosmos within perfect visibility of the disciple. With rare exceptions, certain occult incidents evoked by the Master are indispensable before the aspirant can achieve sufficient clarity of inner vision to gain this ultimate spiritual penetration.

There is a very clear and definite distinction between occultism and mysticism, spiritualism and spirituality. Failure to grasp the full import of this difference can lead only to dire confusion.

While occult phenomena often play an important role in the regeneration of the aspirant, it is essential for him to be aware that, no matter how real they seem, they are no less the product of false imagination than the ordinary phenomena of the gross world. As stepping stones toward the spiritual goal, they are indispensable, as is the rest of the illusory world; but as far as the aspirant is concerned, the instant he perceives God as the ultimate and only Reality, occult phenomena, together with the whole universe of illusion, return to the nothingness in which they had their inception.

Thus, while in profound truth the whole universe and all it represents has no more substance or reality than a zero, the God-realized Master makes legitimate use of his occult powers when he finds it necessary to bring into play the illusory phenomena of an illusory world to help disentangle the mind of an aspirant who had become enmeshed in its delusion. For until he is liberated from the web of this falsehood, the aspirant is incapable of fulfilling his true spiritual mission upon this earth, which is to realize the divine life and to help others do likewise. This can be achieved only by manifesting divine life in every thought and deed, every moment of every day.

To penetrate into the essence of all being, to plumb the significance of creation, to attain integral oneness with the divine symphony of the universe, and to release the fragrance of this sublime attainment for the guidance and benefit of others, by expressing, in the workaday world of forms, the truth, love, purity, and beauty of God's eternal rhythm—this is the sole pursuit that has any intrinsic and absolute worth. All other quests, exertions, and attainments, if divorced from this goal, are of short-lived, perishable importance.

⌒ MEDITATION ⌒

EDITATION MAY BE DESCRIBED as the path that the aspirant cuts for himself while trying to penetrate beyond the limitations of the mind. Intellect plays an important part in the process of meditation, but purely mechanical application of the mind to this task not only becomes irksome but must ultimately lead to failure. To prevent this, the aspirant is well advised to follow the guidance of the Master, who knows the pitfalls and how to avoid them. A few basic suggestions will greatly simplify the work of the disciple and guard him against disappointments.

There are three kinds of meditation. In the first, it is the intellect that is brought predominantly into play; this might be called *discriminative meditation*. In the second, the heart has pride of place; this may be referred to as the *meditation of the heart*. The third type of meditation is pivoted around the active nature of man, and this might rightly be called the *meditation of action*.

Discriminative meditation is exemplified by the mental assertion of an intellectual formula, such as, "I am not my gross, mental, or subtle body; I am without limitation; I am Infinite." The meditation of the heart is expressed by the constant and unhampered flow of love from aspirant to Master—the Divine Beloved. The meditation of action is represented by the unreserved dedication of the aspirant's life to the selfless service of the Master and of humanity.

In the prespiritual stage, meditations are wholly without spiritual motivation. When they are not daydreams, they are in the nature of mental acrobatics; both are almost exclusively concerned with mundane objects and pursuits, disregarding totally the effect they may have upon the spiritual growth of the individual.

The sense of spontaneity experienced in meditations of the prespiritual period is due to the ego-interest created by individual karmic impressions and tendencies. They are, in fact, the crest of the momentum that has its origin in the accumulated impressions and tendencies of the past. They not only are far from being expressions of freedom of action or efforts at liberation, but are actually symptoms of spiritual bondage and tend to further ensnare the individual.

At the prespiritual level, man is engulfed in unrelieved ignorance concerning the goal of infinite freedom; and, though he is far from being happy and contented, he is so deeply identified with karmic interests, so completely enslaved to their appeal, that he experiences gratification in their furtherance. But the pleasure of his chase is conditional and transitory, and the spontaneity that he experiences is illusory, because through all his pursuits his mind is the puppet of his own limitations, the unwitting stooge of his ego, which uses his artificially stimulated eagerness for its own destructive ends.

There may seem to be a resemblance between the true meditation of the spiritually liberated soul and the prespiritual mental exertions of worldly man, but this resemblance is merely superficial; under its thin surface is the vast abyss between the impulsiveness of the ego and the true spontaneity of the spirit; between bondage and freedom, between fleeting pleasure of the senses and abiding happiness of the soul. In prespiritual meditation the operation of the mind is a slave to unconscious compulsion; in the spiritually emancipated, mental activity is the free-choice expression of conscious and unfettered initiative. The two functions are worlds apart.

In the world of the aspirant, meditation plays a purposeful, dynamic part. In all its forms, its sole aim is to attain — directly or indirectly — the complete merging of the mind in divine infinity.

In the early stages it is necessary for the aspirant to make use of the ordinary forms of meditation. Even those in the advanced spiritual state have to resort to most of the specialized forms. Those, however, who are in intimate contact with a God-realized Master can often dispense with many routine and even special forms of meditation. Such is the potency of genuine devotion to the Perfect Master, so infallible his guidance, so mighty the virtue of the disciple's love for the Master and the Master's response, that the irresistible spiritual power generated by them transcends the limitations of time and impediments; it helps achieve directly and in less time what endless forms of meditation, repeated over extended periods of time, strive to accomplish indirectly.

The Master guides the aspirant in the selection of the few types of meditation that will help most to speed his particular progress. He instructs the disciple in the most effective performance of the chosen meditations.

When the mind is thus perfectly tuned to the object of meditation, it merges with the Absolute and experiences a state of spontaneous enjoyment of uninterrupted self-knowledge, in which the aspirant loses his limited individuality and discovers that he is identical with God.

When the soul emerges from the ego-shell and soars into the infinite life of God, its artificial, limited individuality is replaced by the divine Reality of unlimited consciousness. The soul becomes aware of its oneness with God and in that conscious knowledge preserves its divine individuality. Thus individuality is not entirely extinguished; the pure essence of it is retained in spiritualized form.

This state of God-consciousness is infinite in every respect, characterized by unlimited understanding, purity, love, and happiness. To be initiated into this state is to arrive at the endlessness of the life in eternity.

∾ THE LIFE OF THE SPIRIT ∾

THE WAYS OF THE IMPRESSIONABLE MANY are as a rule emblematic of the attitude and behavior of the influential few. In our age, these key figures in public life are, with rare exceptions, glamorous exponents of crass materialism. They are habitually played up by news-hungry front-page exploitation; the inevitable psychological effect is world-consciousness of gross materialism.

Worldly man, in his limited vision, fancies something to be right; he then proceeds to make it right for other people of similar tendencies, and to declare it sacrosanct for those whose concept of right differs from his. Such a life of arbitrary negation and uncritical imitation is not the life of the spirit; blind surrender to convention does not necessarily result in wise action; much less does it lead to perfection. The life of the spirit has its basis in a true understanding of values, and is governed by it.

In the life of perfect action there must be harmonious adjustment between the material and spiritual aspects of life. This cannot be effected by granting equal importance to them. The spirit must and ever will have an inviolable priority over matter. This sovereignty is expressed not by avoiding or rejecting matter, but by making full use of it as an appropriate vehicle for the expression of the spirit.

There is no basic conflict between the current of mundane life and the life of the spirit. The spiritually evolved do not disdain objects of beauty or works of art; they do not disparage the noble achievements of science or scorn the constructive attainments of politics. Things of beauty become degraded when perverted into objects of craving, jealousy, or exclusive possessiveness. Creations of art degenerate into mediums for the inflation of the ego and the breeding of human frailties; triumphs of science are desecrated by man into instruments for mutual destruction; domestic and international chaos is aggravated and perpetuated by the prostitution of politics for selfish ends. Rightly employed and invested with spiritual understanding, however, things of beauty can become a source of purity, inspiration, and joy; works of art have the power to ennoble and raise the consciousness of man; attainments of science reveal their capacity to redeem mankind from unnecessary handicaps and suffering; political action, transmuted by the alchemy of the spirit into statesmanship, can be instrumental in promoting true brotherhood of humanity.

The life of the spirit is not expressed through ignoring worldly spheres of existence. It comes to full flowering when applied to the task of transmuting the material world into a channel for the divine purpose, which is to bring love, peace, happiness, beauty, and spiritual perfection within the reach of all.

The life of the spirit finds its truest expression in all-inclusiveness, free from attachment, in appreciation untrammeled by entanglement. This cosmic poise comes to ultimate fruition in spiritually perfect souls. They have the divine capacity to manifest supreme excellence in any phase of life that they deem necessary for the spiritual quickening of other souls. If there is lack of happiness or beauty or goodness in the lives of those who come within the orbit of the Master, these very deficiencies are transmuted by him into opportunities to shower upon them his divine love and to redeem them from temporal or spiritual poverty. Thus the everyday responses of the Perfect Master to his worldly environment are the highest expressions of the life of the spirit on the earth plane. They are manifestations of dynamic, creative divinity that spreads and multiplies itself, spiritualizing everything with which it comes in contact.

⁓ PERFECTION ⁓

THERE ARE TWO KINDS OF PERFECTION: the comparative perfection of the world of duality, and the absolute perfection of the spirit, which is beyond duality. Like all other aspects of mundane existence, worldly perfection, too, admits of degrees. Good and bad, strength and weakness, virtue and vice, are all opposites of duality, though in truth they are merely different degrees of the one Reality. Evil is the minimum of good, weakness the lowest degree of strength, vice the ebb tide of virtue. Perfection and imperfection in the world of duality are both products of comparison, contrast, and relative interpretation. Perfection assumes meaning in its own right only when it is compared with man's concept of imperfection, and vice versa.

In the nonspiritual concept, perfection is subject not merely to gradation but also to classification. A man may be perfect in science and imperfect in everything else. At the other end of the scale, murder without leaving a clue is referred to as the perfect crime. The differences and degrees of mundane perfection are applicable to every phase of man's existence; they are subject to excellence of quality or extent of capacity, and are all in the domain of the intellect.

Spiritual perfection is of an entirely different kind. It has no parallel in man's world of duality and is entirely beyond the scope of the intellect. The spiritually perfect are conscious of the divine fact that nothing exists but God—the only Reality—and that everything which seems to exist so solidly in the world of duality is only illusion.

Perfection in one field of endeavor is no perfection; it is merely a one-sided exaggeration of a faculty or capacity—an abnormality that actually results in the incapacity to adjust oneself to the ever-changing vicissitudes of life. In the rare instances when the one-sided perfectionist has a chance to function in an environment that gives full scope to his particular capacity, he may enjoy a fleeting sense of harmony with the world and even achieve a temporary state of false happiness. But the moment he is taken out of his environment and placed in an atmosphere that makes demands on his lesser faculties, his poise is shattered, and he generally becomes the victim of an acute sense of failure and frustration. Perfection in merely one aspect of life then becomes an impediment rather than an advantage.

True perfection implies the ultimate in every respect—a perfection in which all the aspects of man's total capacity are fully developed. It does not merely transcend the opposites; it also includes them. The truly perfect man is not bound by any arbitrary rule or limited ideal; he responds with absolute spontaneity and in perfect rhythm to all the possible situations in life. He can adapt himself instantly to the most unexpected changes in fortune or to the most startling variations in environment, without for a moment surrendering the spiritual poise that is the balance wheel of his being. He maintains an unshakable sense of harmony, an imperturbable spirit of peace baffling to the uninitiated. The perfect man is all-perfect, but no matter in what field of endeavor he is called upon to exercise his perfection, he functions with utter detachment. Like a person with gloves who handles dirt without being soiled by it, the spiritually perfect man can be engaged in worldly activities without being affected or bound by them. Such perfection is beyond the limitations of worldly concepts; it can be achieved only through spiritual emancipation, which is tantamount to God-realization.

Perfection in the truest sense does not belong to God as God, nor does it belong to man as man; perfection manifests when man becomes God or when God becomes man. It comes into being when the finite transcends its limitations and realizes its infinity, or when the Infinite discards His apparent aloofness and becomes a man. In either case, the finite and the Infinite do not function outside each other. Perfection is achieved when there is a happy and conscious blending of the finite and the Infinite. In such a blissful integration the Infinite reveals Himself through the finite, without thereby being limited; the finite transcends its sense of limitation in the full knowledge of being the revelation of the Infinite.

⌒ MASTER AND DISCIPLE ⌒

THOSE WHO ARE UNCONSCIOUS of their divinity can have no concept of the God-state; they are aware only of the body-state. To achieve the God-state, they have to love, with their whole being, a Perfect Master who dwells constantly in the God-state; they have to dedicate themselves to him and be guided by him. The Master is supremely impersonal; his only concern at all times is to remove the veils between the limited consciousness of the disciple and his Higher Self. There can be no conflict between the devotion of the disciple to his Master and his allegiance to his own Higher Self. On the contrary, at the end of his search the disciple discovers that the Master is none other than his own Higher Self in another form.

The Master in his utter impersonality and unimpeded divinity is so perfectly complete that he has no desires for himself. All that the Master requires of the disciple is that he reconstitute himself in light of the higher Truth. To become the disciple of a God-realized Master is to begin to tread the path that leads to the ultimate spiritual goal. This is the meaning and purpose of true discipleship.

The aspirant has to climb his own path; the Master's province is to confirm, bring into focus, and consolidate the previously developed intuitions and perceptions of the aspirant, and to precipitate his consciousness into the next stage, which, though indispensable, cannot, by its very nature, be anticipated by the disciple, nor comprehended by him until he has reached it.

Since the Master is for the aspirant a symbol of the supreme self-in-all, he finds the problem of true adjustment to the Master identical with the problem of realizing his own inner divinity and arriving at true adjustment to all other forms of the Supreme Self. Through his allegiance to the Master the aspirant gives effect to his growing appreciation of the funda-mental unity of all these problems. From the point of view of psychological strategy, the aspirant through his discipleship is in a position to tackle these problems not as separate phenomena but as aspects of one problem. Thus he can arrive at true integration, which is totally different from a temporary compromise between conflicting claims. In order to help the disciple achieve this difficult task, the Master becomes the nucleus of all the spiritual idealism of the aspirant; thus the Master helps bring about the intensive concentration of psychic energy that the disciple must develop in order to break through the many barriers that lie between him and his goal.

Obedience to the Master, implied in full self-surrender, is of two kinds: intellectual and absolute. Of these, intellectual obedience comes first and is preliminary to absolute obedience, which, however, is more fruitful. Next to all—love for the Master, unquestioned obedience to him is the most potent step in the right direction that the disciple could possibly make. It is obedience without reservations, not even bound by the requirement that the real significance of the Master's orders be within the intellectual comprehension of the devotee.

Through such implicit and unquestioning obedience, all the tangled knots of the disciple's desires, tendencies, and complex life impressions are unraveled, released, and dissolved. The deep link created between Master and aspirant through such unqualified obedience makes possible an unhindered, never-ending flow of spiritual wisdom and power from Master to pupil.

⌇ GOD-REALIZATION ⌇

To arrive at true self-knowledge is to arrive at the realization of God. God-realization is a unique experience. It is different from all other states of consciousness because they are realized through the medium of the mind, whereas God-consciousness in no way depends upon the mind or any other human channel. To know anything other than one's own self is possible only through some limited intermediary; to know one's own self, no finite medium is necessary.

In God-realization the soul has discarded its delusion of separateness; it has transcended duality in the crowning realization of its identity with Infinite Reality. In the achievement of God-realization, the shackles of limited individuality have forever been broken; man's world of shadows has vanished; the veils of illusion have been permanently lifted; the feverishness and agonizing distress that are so inseparable from the pursuits of limited consciousness have been supplanted by the tranquillity and bliss of Truth-consciousness; and the restlessness and fury of temporal existence have become completely resolved in the ineffable peace and unfathomed stillness of eternity.

⌒ THE GOD-MAN ⌒

IN THE ORDINARY MAN OF THE WORLD, the limited individuality is identified with a finite name and form predominates; its mundane activities create a veil of ignorance that completely obscures the God within. Before this veil can be lifted, the limited individual has to surrender his limited existence. When the "I" disappears without leaving a trace of its limited ego-life, what remains is God. Surrender of the limited life is the relinquishing of the firmly rooted delusion of separate existence. It is not the giving up of anything real; it is the discarding of the false and the inheritance of the True.

The soul in bondage is tied to the world of forms by the chain of karmic experiences, tendencies, and obligations, which create and sustain the identification of the soul with the illusory bodies of man. The conflict and disharmony within consciousness, and the perversions in the expression of man's will, arise out of this false identification, rather than merely out of physical, subtle, and mental body consciousness.

Not until the moment of God-realization on the seventh and final plane of spiritual ascension does this mortal conflict come to an end. Then at last the soul comes into full possession of its own divine joy, which is utterly beyond the comprehension of the nonrealized. It is an eternal bliss unparalleled in mundane experience, yet it does not unbalance the soul, for it is now permanently balanced in the poise of nonduality. No longer is the soul subject to the ebb and flow of newly found love and joy—and the inevitable disillusionment and sorrow that follow in their wake. The ecstasy of the moments of God-proximity and the heartbreak of long intervals of retrogression are over too, for the soul is now one with the Divine Beloved, completely merged in Him; it is one with God, *itself* now the infinite ocean of unbounded happiness.

The happiness of the God-realized is without limitations and is self-sustaining; it is eternally at its highest peak, not subject to fluctuation; with God-realization comes unqualified finality, and unassailable equanimity.

The happiness of the saints is born of increasing proximity and closer intimacy with the Divine Beloved, from whom they are, however, still separated. The God-realized are one with the Divine Beloved; their happiness is an inalienable aspect of the God-state itself, with which they are identical, and in which there is no duality. The happiness of the saints is derivative; the happiness of the God-realized is self-emanating. The happiness of the saints owes its inception and growth to the increasing influx of divine grace; the happiness of the God-realized has no beginning and no end; it simply is.

One who has realized his identity with the Infinite is the God-man. The God-man is free from all karmic ties; he is liberated from consciousness of the various body states; he uses these illusory outer forms merely as instruments for the expression of the divine will in its undefiled purity, like the master violinist who expresses on his Stradivarius every nuance of the composer's inspiration, without identifying himself with it.

The God-man has realized the ultimate Truth. He knows the true nature of God and is aware of the true nature of creation. His purified consciousness has revealed to him that creation, in fact, does not exist; that it is merely the changing shadow of God, who is the Only Eternal, Real existence, who is at the heart of all creation, who is All-Creation Himself.

The state of perfection in which the God-man dwells is beyond all forms of duality and opposites; it is a state of untarnished divinity and boundless freedom, immortal sweetness and undying joy, perfect completeness and unhampered creativeness.

The God-man is inseparably and forever united with God. He dwells in a state of nonduality in the very midst of duality. He not only knows himself to be one with all, but also knows himself to be the Only One. The God-man, no longer separate from the One, but All-One himself, sees all souls as his own and himself in everything. His universal mind includes all minds in its scope. Although he knows himself to be identical with God and is thus eternally free, he also knows himself to be one with all souls in bondage and is thus vicariously bound. Though he constantly experiences the eternal bliss of God-realization, he also experiences suffering by proxy, because of the agony of unrealized souls, with whom he knows himself to be one. This is the true meaning of the crucifixion of Christ. The God-man is forever being crucified and continuously taking birth.

The God-man is the Lord and Servant of the universe at one and the same time. As one who showers his spiritual bounty on all in measureless abundance, he is the Lord of the universe; as one who continuously bears the burden of all and helps them through endless spiritual difficulties, he is the Servant of the universe.

Just as he is Lord and Servant in one, he is also the supreme Lover and the matchless Beloved in one. The love he gives and receives is the divine galvanizer that frees the soul from the inertia of ignorance. In giving love, the God-man gives it to himself in other forms; in receiving it, he reabsorbs what has been awakened through his own grace: the blessing that he continuously showers on all without distinction. The grace of the God-man is like rain, which falls equally on all the land, whether barren or fertile, but fructifies only those acres that have been rendered fertile by arduous and patient toil.

The banyan tree grows huge and mighty, giving free shade and shelter to travelers, protecting them from sun, rain, and storm. In the fullness of its growth, its descending branches strike their roots deep into the yielding earth to seed other banyan trees, which, in due course, not only become as huge and mighty as their parent, spreading their benevolence of shade and shelter to travelers, but also inherit the power to re-create themselves in similar full-grown banyan trees.

The God-man is the divine banyan tree—shelter and protection to wandering souls, creator of other God-men—whose work is done without thought of recompense or expectation of reward.

In the God-man, the divine purpose of creation has been completely realized. He no longer has anything to obtain for himself by remaining in the world, yet he retains his outer form. In divine compassion he continues to use it for the emancipation of other souls, to help them attain God-consciousness. The voluntary presence of the God-man on the earth plane is the highest demonstration of divine love in action.

⌒ THE AVATAR ⌒

T HE DIVINE FREEDOM from earthly limitations that comes to man with God-realization assumes three forms. Most God-realized souls leave the body at once and forever, and remain eternally merged in the unmanifest aspect of God. They are conscious only of the immortal bliss of union with the Infinite. Creation no longer exists for them. Their constant round of births and deaths is ended. They have achieved final liberation from the body.

Some God-realized souls retain the body for a time and remain on earth, but their consciousness is merged completely in the unmanifest aspect of God. They are therefore not conscious of either their bodies or creation. They constantly experience the infinite bliss, power, and knowledge of God, but they cannot consciously use these in creation, nor can they help others to attain liberation. Nevertheless they are focal points on earth for the concentration and radiation of the infinite power, knowledge, and bliss of God.

A few God-realized souls retain their bodies, yet are conscious of themselves as God in both His unmanifest and manifest aspects. They know themselves as God-in-all and are therefore able to render spiritual help to all souls, under all conditions, and to assist those who are ready to attain God-realization. These are the Perfect Masters.

There are fifty-six Perfect Masters in the world at all times. They are always one in consciousness, always different in function. As a rule they live and work incognito, apart from the general public; but five, who act in a sense as a directing body, always work in public and in an atmosphere of commanding prominence. In Avataric periods, the Avatar, as the Perfect Master Supreme, takes his place at the head of this body and of the spiritual hierarchy as a whole.

Avataric periods are like the springtide of creation. They bring a new release of power, a new awakening of consciousness, a new experience of life—not merely for a few, but for all. Qualities of energy and awareness that had been used and enjoyed between Avataric periods by only a few advanced souls are made available for all humanity. Life as a whole is stepped up to a new rate of vibration. The transition from sensation to reason was one such step; the transition from reason to intuition will be another.

This new influx of the creative impulse takes place through the medium of a divine personality, a supreme incarnation of God—an Avatar. The Avatar was the first individual soul to emerge from the evolutionary process as the Perfect Master Supreme; he is the only Avatar who has ever manifested or ever will manifest. Through him, God first completed the journey from unconscious divinity to conscious divinity—first unconsciously became man in order to consciously become God. Through the Avatar, God, at His own ordained intervals of time, consciously becomes man for the liberation of mankind.

The Avatar appears in different forms under different names, at different times, in different parts of the world. As his appearance always coincides with the spiritual renaissance of mankind, so the time immediately preceding his manifestation is always one in which humanity suffers from the pangs of the approaching birth. At such periods man seems more than ever enslaved by desire, more than ever driven by greed, held by fear, swept by anger, and engulfed in carnage. The strong dominate the weak, the rich oppress the poor, large masses of people are exploited for the benefit of the few who are in power. The individual, who finds no peace or rest, seeks to forget himself in excitement. Immorality increases, crime flourishes, and God is ridiculed. Corruption spreads throughout the social order. Racial, class, and national hatreds are aroused and fostered. Wars break out, and humanity grows desperate. There seems to be no possibility of stemming the tide of destruction.

At this moment the Avatar appears. The supreme manifestation of God in human form, he is the divine gauge by which man may measure his own true size and glimpse the height of his ultimate growth. By the perfection of his divinely human life upon this earth, the Avatar inspires a complete revaluation of man's worldly standards of existence.

In those who contact him, he awakens a love that consumes all selfish desires in the flame of the one desire to serve him. Those who consecrate their lives to him gradually become identified with him in consciousness.

Little by little their humanity is absorbed into his divinity, and they become free.

Those who are closest to him are known as his Circle. Every Perfect Master has an intimate Circle of twelve disciples who, in point of realization, are made equal to the Master himself, though they differ from him in function and authority. In Avataric periods, the Avatar has a Circle of one hundred and twenty disciples, all of whom experience realization and work for the liberation of others.

The Avatar awakens contemporary humanity to a realization of its true spiritual nature, gives liberation to those who are ready, and quickens the life of the spirit in his time. For posterity is left the stimulating power of his divinely human example, the nobility of a life supremely lived, of a love unmixed with desire, of a power unused except for others, of a peace untroubled by ambition, of a knowledge undimmed by illusion. He has demonstrated the possibility of a divine life for all humanity: a heavenly life upon earth. Those who have the necessary courage, integrity, and readiness can follow when they will.

∿ BLENDING WITH THE MASTER ∿

HE WHO WOULD REALIZE ME MUST HAVE:

Intense longing for union with Me
Unfailing humility
Insatiable spiritual hunger
Unquestionable faith
Imperturbable self-control
Unwavering fidelity
Impregnable peace of mind

HE MUST DEDICATE HIS LIFE TO:

Unconditional renunciation
Spontaneous obedience
Whole-hearted surrender
Unselfish service
Self-giving love

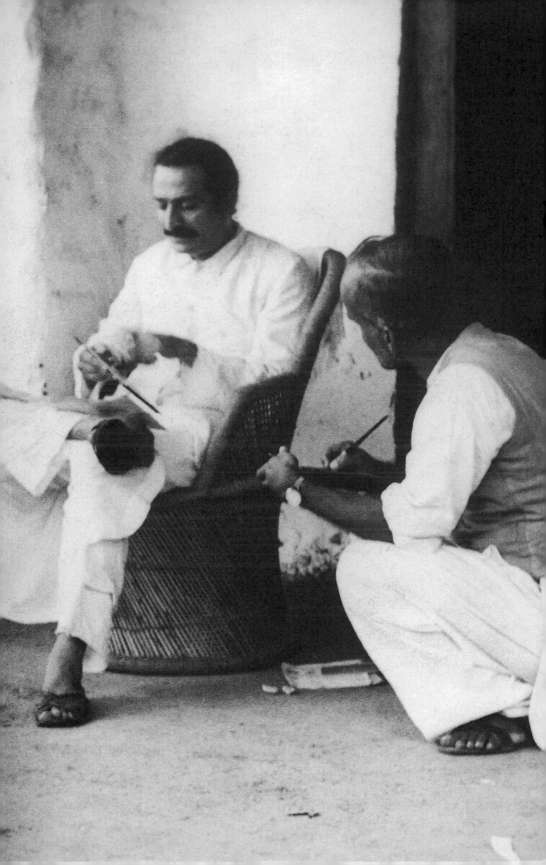

THE BELOVED ANSWERS

Conversations with Meher Baba

Most of the interviews with Meher Baba were brief and to the point.
The method was simple. Those who wished to ask questions did so
through an interpreter who understood Baba's finger signs and gestures.
Baba answered each question and at times explained in detail. There were
some who came to Baba to feel his "touch" and to receive a "spiritual push."
All who came to him were assured of his help and guidance.

She is a painter.

I am also a painter. I paint the hearts of people with colors of spirituality. She is a good soul.

She feels she has a guilty heart.

No, she is not guilty as she believes. Everyone has weaknesses, but it is the heart that counts. She need not worry. I will help her spiritually.

Would you help me to understand the process of evolution?

Yes, I will. It is the process of evolution through which a soul has to pass to attain the human form to realize the Truth, and human beings also have to experience suffering to realize God, which is the goal of humanity and of eternal happiness.

[To a visitor who is paralyzed:]

It is not the paralysis of the body that matters, but of the mind that retards the soul…Yoga practices do not matter much…he has to learn much to progress spiritually. I will help him spiritually.

With my own language I speak with God, because I love Truth.

Love for Truth is everything, hence there is no need of speaking anything.

I cannot imagine how people can be anti-God.

It's only due to delusion. Once this disappears, they understand.

༄

Are you happy?

No, very, very miserable.

Try to be always happy. Never think that "life is dreadful"; "I am tired of life"; such thoughts really make life miserable. "Life is worth living" —if you think like that, all difficulties will appear insignificant. I will help you try to develop love. Never think, "I am alone, I have so much to do, I am poor," and so on. All are poor. The whole world is poor. Even the millionaires are poor, because they have greed and want more. Do not worry. My blessings.

Meher Baba is handed over a written statement by an elderly man. It is his confession of the confused state of his life, which makes him believe that he is fallen and feels utterly broken.

> *I know. No need to tell me, I will explain. Don't worry. When one is meant for spiritual advancement, one has either love or lust in him to the extreme. This lust must be converted into love. What is lust but a craving to satisfy physical senses?—and love is the craving of the soul. I know all about you and will spiritually help you. Never think that you have fallen so as not to rise again. Does he want to ask anything more?*

He thanks you very much. He got the answer that he wanted, and feels much relieved.

∿

> *Ask her if she wants to speak about anything to me.*

[She nods refusal.]

> *I understand, because what can explanations mean when internal help is at hand? Real help is spiritual help, and not by words and explanations. I will help her.*

[A tear trickles down her cheek. She places her hand in Baba's, and sits there for about a minute. When Baba asks her to leave, she goes away overwhelmed.]

∿

He is a dancer and is very glad to see you.

> *Dancing is a very good art if expressed rightly. It has divine qualities, and if properly expressed, it will have a wonderful effect. If expressed improperly, it has the opposite effect... I am happy to see you.*

I feel so happy, too.

> *Any other question?*

For some time now, he does not quite clearly understand his own individual way of doing things, the right way to express himself through art.

Soon you will know. I will help you spiritually. You will feel it. This contact will help you henceforth.

⌇

Any questions?

What he craves is the contact. Words are therefore unnecessary.

Yes, it is true. If it is true that I know everything, then there is no need to ask me any questions and explanations. And if you feel I do not know, what is the use of asking me?—for then I would not be able to help you.

He has no doubt about your powers and knowledge.

I will help him spiritually. I like him very, very much.

He has gone through terrible times and struggle.

I know. He has a very good heart, and my help will make him understand things as they are.

⌇

Nervous? Tell her to be rested.

She is in love with a church pianist and asks if that friendship is to be kept up very pure.

Where is the harm to keep it up?

Catholic law prevents marriage with a man who is divorced. The Church is against it …That is the conflict.

But do they love each other?

Yes.

Then love is all that matters, if there is no lust. I see no harm in it. Let that love grow so that it makes two souls as one. I will spiritually help her to make this love grow purer.

How can one develop a conscience to attune oneself to Truth?

Conscience can never be defined as right or wrong, because it is not based on intellect. So when one feels, the emotional side is affected.

Is it something internal?

Today your conscience might say to believe in me, and tomorrow it might say not to believe. Conscience means the immediate response of the emotions, and so always do what you feel. If you feel today to believe in me, do believe. Tomorrow if you don't feel, don't. Conscience is different from discrimination.

Is there something higher than conscience or discrimination?

Yes, higher than discrimination is divine love, and when one really loves, conscience and discrimination are out of place. Everything is immaterial then; nothing counts.

~

She is a student of law.

And law is good. All this universe is based on the divine law of love, which encompasses all existence. I will spiritually help her to understand more.

How can I strive to achieve in life what one wants materially and also lasting permanently?

Yes, it can be done. What does perfection mean if it does not include material life? It is easy and practical. One has only to adopt that life which keeps materialism and spirituality in balance. How to do that? Lead the worldly life, attend to all your worldly duties, but for some moments in the day, long to know something that is beyond life. This longing will increase gradually, and that will make you free and detached from material results.

~

She has come to ask to develop the divine within. She feels she cannot achieve it herself without help.

She will…with my help. Never be disheartened. It is all within, and I will help you to open it. I am so happy to see her longing for spiritual attainment.

She asks for nothing else.

I am so happy to know this.

How can spirituality be attained?

It cannot be attained by the intellect, but by heart and feeling and inner experience. I could explain for hours, but that would be nothing compared to one second of my internal help. Do one thing. Every night, just before retiring, think for one minute, "The Infinite God is within me, and I am part of the Infinite." This will connect her more and more with me internally.

~

She says she doesn't want to bother you with questions.

That is the real thing, to know me through inner feeling.

She always had a great longing to meet you.

[Baba makes her sit beside him, and she gives her hand in his.]

She wanted so much to be near you.

I know how she feels. I will help her.

~

Anything to ask?
I cannot ask anything. I am so perplexed.
> *And it is a pity. I have not much time, because when one comes,*
> *I must explain. But for that I must have time. Anyway, you can ask.*
> *I would like to make you sit here and think of questions.*

But it makes it so awkward for you.
> *Never mind, go on.*

I am very anxious to find something real that we have to think of and do.
> *And that something is the only thing worth having. I will help*
> *you spiritually.*

Can I have that?
> *Yes, you can. It is not through words or explanations that it can be*
> *explained. It is within you. It is to be opened. I will do it.*

~

In New York, I saw some of your people who made me think and feel
that I must have something else to seek, and for that I do try to see that
Reality.
> *And when you find it, you can experience [higher] things even while*
> *being involved in worldly affairs. Every morning, the moment you*
> *get up, think for a minute, "It is in me," and rest assured that I will*
> *help you.*

I understand, very well. I realize and believe it. I thank you very much
for all that you have given me already and am sure I will be helped.

~

She doesn't dream or think of Jesus.
> *Why bother about the physical Christ?…If she can't visualize as clearly*
> *as she wants to, she can feel the Christ within. That means the ideal or*
> *Pure Love.*

She has read the Sermon on the Mount but can't have a clear concept of Jesus.

I will help her. Do one thing. Immediately when she gets up every morning, just let her have this thought: "Christ is within me," and leave the rest to me. I will help her spiritually.

Anything to ask?

[She just looks at Baba.]

And in reality, from the spiritual viewpoint there is never a need of explanations. It is to be felt and experienced. One can, by reading books and having theories, get some intellectual understanding of Truth, but that is not real understanding. One must experience Truth, be able to live Truth, and realize Truth.

Is it difficult?

Very easy, if one takes it to mind.

How?

So easy, but people make it so complicated that it seems like a gigantic task. I will tell you. Think much of others and very little of yourself. Just try. When you have a scarf and she [pointing to a lady] needs one, spare your scarf for her. Even if she has something more, and you nothing, don't feel it. This is a simile. Don't take it literally. It is also simple. I will help you spiritually. Think less of yourself.

How can one be a good doctor and use that science best?

It is very simple. Through love. If you love your work, you can do it with love, and anything that is done with love has perfect results. To be a good doctor, always have in mind that to you all patients, good or bad, big or small, are equal. Treat a beggar with as much care and interest as you would a millionaire, and in case you find that you are not paid the price, you must not for a moment think of refusing treatment. It is simple and practical, and yet a good many doctors don't observe this simple rule. Only if a doctor realizes that one infinite God is within all, then that doctor works like a saint! I am a doctor of souls. To me, good and bad, all are lovable and I help each according to the need. But although it is simple for you to be good doctor, it is very difficult to practice it. So many things interfere — reputation, name, money, society, circumstances, and so on. You can be a good doctor if you take it to mind.

Master, thank you very much for all you have said. I will try to act accordingly.

~

Anything to ask?

Why do you not bring salvation now?

The world needs it very badly, but still there is a need for some of its greater evils to be eradicated, and then it will be very soon. I know it, because I work it out.

Will salvation be felt by anybody and everybody?

Mostly by all, but in degrees. To some more, to others less, but it will be a universal spiritual push.

Why does not everybody find or feel God within?

It is nobody's fault. Every soul, sooner or later, has to realize the God within.

Why do a few realize God and many do not?

It is because these many have yet to pass through the experiences of duality [Maya, or illusion] and because to reach unity one has to pass through duality. It is like this. [Meher Baba draws a diagram of one point with two branches shooting out of it and then becoming one again.] These two branches are virtue and vice, good and bad; they are aspects of duality. I will help you.

〜

It is so puzzling to see why at times when one desires good, bad comes out; then the confusion. Must one feel responsible for bad results of good work?

It is essential to desire good.

She has to speak to people, she believes, who are worthy to be helped; but they do not listen to her, and the results are painful. That's what she feels.

Always think of helping and not of results. Never worry about results, because selfless service means trying to help others without thinking that "I am doing this or that."

The world and others reproach her for her good motives.

Always work with all your heart, hoping for the best, and don't worry. The world crucified Christ.

She has the strength to fight it all, but still worries for others.

The fighting is good, but worrying is unnecessary. Remember what I have told you; try to follow it, and I will help you spiritually.

〜

Can one realize virtue without experiencing vice?

One has to experience both, virtue and vice, to be able to realize the Infinite, who is beyond both.

Is Christ the only question of realization?

Yes, Christ is to be realized.

Is there any great difference between Christ and church religion?

A world of difference. Christ is to be lived and not "ceremonized" [found in ceremonies].

Is this path-finding more difficult in the West than in the East?

No. It is a different outlook, because in the East as in the West there are intellectual giants. Also in both there are good hearts. And in the teachings of great men, both East and West, there is love; only the name and method are differently expressed.

I understand. Thank you for clearing the mist.

~

Happy to see you.

He is an artist who has encountered opposition and is trying to find a clear way in the face of it all.

There lies the fun of the game—to meet opposition, to face and encounter it. If not, life becomes dull and monotonous. One can find spirituality only through opposition. But when you are facing it, if you are determined, it becomes enduring, just like a wall which stands erect, unaffected, against any number of balls thrown at it; the balls rebound with the same force with which they are struck against the wall. On encountering opposition, life becomes enduring, determined, and unaffected, like the wall that stands erect and unaffected against the continued strikes of the ball thrown against it. And art is a divine thing. It can only be rightly expressed if opposed, to bring out its inner beauty that lies behind. I will help you spiritually.

~

How could I know the state "beyond," which I consider to be the goal of life?

Try and practice to keep the mind blank.

I try to curb my desires—say, smoking. I can control for a time, but they rise up again and overpower me.

By daily dwelling on the thought and trying to keep the mind blank, these desires will be diminished gradually and eliminated eventually, and in this process of your trying to do this, you will feel my help.

Oh, will I? [After a moment's pause] I have been trying so hard to bring the mind to a state of coma, but the rush of thoughts and the unsteadiness of mind make things very difficult, and I feel it is impossible.

It is possible by observing the correct method of control. The disturbing thoughts should be allowed to come and go. There is no need to try to exercise a direct pressure to drive them away. The more you do so, the more they will confront you. So keep an attitude of apathy and total indifference, holding the "central" intended thought uppermost in mind, disregarding every other disturbing thought. [Here Baba gives her a certain process to practice every day.] You will feel my help, which I shall release at the time. This contact will help you a great deal, as you will realize in the future.

∽

I am so happy to see you…I am so tired of life and very unhappy… I don't see how I can improve.

Everyone is unconsciously tired of this life, because everyone seeks happiness but knows not how to get it. But life is so beautiful. It is meant to be happy. I will help you. Then things will appear changed. You will see it. It is always the outlook that counts, and not the object. Today you feel tired, upset, seeing nothing beautiful in things around you in life. If tomorrow you do not feel bored, but cheerful, in the same things that appeared so black to you yesterday…it is all due to changed mentality and outlook. The easy way is not to make much of things. Take them lightly. Say to yourself, "I am meant to be happy, to make others happy," and gradually you do become happy yourself and make others happy too. Don't suggest to your mind, "I am tired, haggard, depressed." That will make you feel worse. Always say, "All is well and beautiful. I will be happy." I will help you spiritually. I can and I will. You will feel it.

∽

Wonderful soul.
[She stares at Meher Baba.]
   Does she want to ask anything?

What must I do for a better life with my mother, who does not approve of what I do for you and for your work?
   Think more of her and less of yourself. That will make matters better; because even if you think at times that your mother is in the wrong and you are in the right, or sometimes that she is in the right and you are in the wrong, still it matters little if you think of her, and not only about her but also about all others in the same way. In short, just think less of yourself and more of others. Real happiness is to make others happy.

[The words make a deep impression on her. After a moment's silence, Baba adds:]
   Very dear soul, I will help you spiritually. My love is pure and infinite.

Thank you very much. I am so happy to have met you. Should I tell my mother regarding my feelings for you?
   Yes, but not for a few days. Later on you can. You will feel. I will tell you somehow.

~

   Anything to ask?
She is in very awkward situations, fight within and fight without, disease, difficulties in profession. She feels that she fails every day.
[She cries with her hand in his.]
   I know it all and will help her. [She sobs.] Yes, I will help you.

She wants to believe in you and have faith in you.
   Yes, she will feel my help. Now that she has met me, it will gradually change her outlook on life.

She believes in you but does not believe in herself.
   My help will make her believe in herself too, and that's the most

beautiful thing in life [to have confidence in one's own self].

How?
> *Because the entire outlook is changed, and I will change it, so that all these difficulties will gradually fade away.*

Can that really be done?
> *Yes. I know that I will help her to gain what I said, and everything will change.*

Is she condemned to be alone, as she feels now?
> *No. When the outlook is changed, she won't feel alone at all.*

&

Very glad to have met you.
> *Anything to ask?*

How can one achieve one's ambition? He [pointing to her son]
is an artist.
> *And art is one of the sources through which the soul expresses itself and inspires others. But to express art thoroughly, one must have the inner emotions opened completely. If you feel something checks you from expressing yourself, then you have to do one thing—that is, to adjust your mental attitude. Just before expressing, think, "I can and will express it thoroughly," and every time you express it, you will find you are more convinced of your expression. It is the mind that keeps it closed. There are many actors who either through inferiority complex or through nervousness or through dryness feel they cannot express, and this [negative] feeling of the mind checks the expression. While acting, think that you are one of the greatest actors of the world, and try to express yourself thoroughly. I will help you spiritually. Just think you are the greatest [actor]. Where's the harm in thinking like that? It is not for pride that you do it, but for bringing the best out of you. There is nothing wrong.*

She feels unhappy being unable to help others as she wants on account of doubts arising in her mind.

She can't help if doubts come into her mind. This feeling of not being able to help others is in itself spiritual.

Can one attain to perfection immediately after coming in contact with a Master?

In some cases, yes. In others, it [progress] is very gradual. It all depends on internal help. It does not necessarily mean that coming into contact with me will make you realized at once. If that were the case, the Jews who were near Jesus all the time and in his immediate contact would not have crucified him. You will understand. I will help you spiritually.

It is a torture to feel one is hard up, unable to help or do anything by way of service to others.

This is very noble. She will be as she wants. Let that desire remain, and she will improve. This contact will help her. My blessings.

~

He is an artist.

I love artists because through art one can express oneself beautifully.

So far, through ideas, he tried to find the source. Is there any other way to find the way to the divine? He has painted fine paintings for a church, with deep insight to approach the subject, and not for competition.

Yes, he has a right to understand and express. Art, when inspired with love, leads to higher realms, and that art will open for you the inner life. When you paint, you forget everything except your object. When you are engrossed in it, you are lost in it; when you are lost in it, your ego diminishes; and when the ego diminishes, Love Infinite appears; and when love is created, God is attained. So you see how art can lead one to find Infinite God.

He realizes that he has his ego, which he must use in a selfless way
to express the Divine.

*Then that ego is not finite and limited. It is then the selfless,
unlimited ego.*

But this he will always try to develop more and more, even through art,
and then leave it to you.

Yes, and I will help him spiritually.

He is sorry to have spoken too much.

*No, don't worry. I am so glad. He has a very good heart. He will have
and feel my help.*

❧

I have seen in the present day in Switzerland, as elsewhere in Europe,
movements in which only a few know things and the masses do not.
They simply follow blindly. I see good in everything.

*It is all right, because the Infinite One is in everything and can be
expressed in everything.*

But isn't happiness the goal of life?

*That is the true aim of life—to attain to real happiness, and it does
not matter through what medium it is attained.*

I understand the words in the Bible, "Love your friends and foes alike…"

*Yes, but it all depends on just one thing: forgetting self-interest.
For those who have no self-interest, even hell is heaven!*

I know that it is through the Master that one attains to Perfection.
But there are other means too, I believe.

*Yes, but that also will gradually have a solution, because it is like
a seesaw. When one end goes up, the other must go down.*

Masters lead, but also mislead.

That is what I said [in connection with the seesaw]; it will happen when the new feeling starts to influence the masses to discriminate, and not be blindly led by emotional people. It is the masses who have to be made to understand, and the time is near.

He is desperate about the masses being labeled on the word of a man and being misled into chaos, as is exactly done at present.

It will all end soon. I feel it infinitely more than you do.

I believe that some power must guide the world aright.

I know. It will happen soon.

You have got the Master of the East to bring new consciousness and happiness; but in the West too, there are means such as art, science, through which they can find heavenly bliss.

It is due to the times [of the spiritual upheaval]. The consciousness desired will come, soon.

∾

I am very happy to see you.

Anything to say?

About the children for whose salvation she strives against the will of the parents and conventional ideas.

Tell her to try conscientiously. I will help her. She must never be afraid of anything or anyone when doing something for the benefit of others. If she wants to develop more and more, tell her to do one thing: let her mind not think too much of her doing it. When doing any service to others, she should not remind them too much of her doing it. She has a noble heart, and I will help her.

She is not physically capable. Will she be able to do her duties?
She wants to.
Yes.

She has an offer to go to America to work in her capacity.
You may go on with the present work as you are now doing; later on, go to America. You have much to do here. Even if you can help one soul, it is enough.

~

He has translated and published your books in German and hopes they will have very good circulation. He feels that the Swiss are not so receptive to Eastern lore. He has published other works too, but the people do not seem to take much interest in them.
Yes, but now they will have to. The internal spiritual message of love will reach every heart, because it is the same Infinite One in the Swiss, in the German, as in all people. It should be unlocked and opened. My love will do that.

Will it affect the materialistic world of the West as it will to the spirituality of the East?
Yes, because when the turning point arrives, those who are more materialistic will feel a greater impact, and so they will also have the same effect. It is like a seesaw.

~

Will world conditions take a better turn?
Yes, it has to.

Will there be an understanding between the East and the West?
Yes, it is inevitable. Soon there will be a worldwide spiritual revolution, and all will have to unite.

Will it be a new religion or a union of all religions into one?

Yes, all will be one. It will just be a movement of eternal love, and so it will be a religion of love.

Same as Christ's?

This change will soon happen in this generation and will last very long. It will be very soon when the spiritual revolution will take place.

Will it express itself through war?

It might or might not. But it will express itself just after an economic war all the world over. I am trying to avert the war [fighting and bloodshed].

How can we help avoid the war? How can we be useful?

By thinking that there will be no war. My millions of agents are working towards that. Your love messages can reach anyone, anywhere; because in all of them there is the one Infinite God. I will help you spiritually.

❧

From the Christian standpoint, Christ is the only one and unique amongst prophets. Do you believe that?

Unique, indeed, from the standpoint of his state and consciousness. The Muslims claim that Muhammad is the only prophet. The Buddhists claim Buddha; the Parsis, Zoroaster; and the Christians, Christ. Each say that their perfect ideal [of the Prophet] is the unique one, but why bother about that? What do names matter? What is important is the life that Jesus lived. To understand Christ, to know him, one has to live his life. Mere ceremonies and talks, discussions, and criticisms don't help one towards knowing Christ. Christ taught one simple thing, love, and so few of his followers have that love developed.

Is this standpoint of "Love" consistent with Christian dogma?

Love has in it selfless service and renunciation of low desires. Pure love includes everything. If one loves, all other low qualities automatically dissolve themselves; and by love, I mean pure love, not sexual love as it is meant today in the world of matter.

This kind of love is impossible without the help of Masters.

Yes. God is within and without. Why not seek Him within? If one seeks the grace of God, and God is not able to give it, what kind of God do you call Him? People talk, but do not seek His grace. It is all one. God is Infinite, the Soul of souls, and the individual souls are the drops of that Infinite Ocean. All this only depends on outlook. You see this [pointing to a flower] as a "flower"; I see it as "God."

Very happy to have seen you, and very grateful for all you have explained.

∾

Happy to see you. [Feels somewhat nervous.]

Do not feel nervous. Anything to ask or say?

I have doubts between you and me, and also why Western religion calls the Eastern confusing and not straight, as of Christ.

And the Eastern people say the same about Western religion. Everyone thinks his own religion is best. This is ignorance. Jesus never meant that. What does religion mean? To find God within. What did Jesus teach? To find him within and not to carry on wars as his own followers have been doing.

How can we realize that?

Through love and helping others selflessly. It is very easy if you think less of yourself and more of others. No matter if you doubt me or do not even believe in me, I will help you.

I want to believe in you and have faith in you.

But why? If what you want is within, you will find it only there. And my need [to help] is only to help you find it, whether you follow me or not.

But it is difficult.

> *I will help you even if you don't want it. When the sun is high up and you feel hot, you cannot avoid it. It does shine on you even if you don't want it to. It is a question of going out of your way to help others, and that I will do. This contact will help you immensely. My blessings.*

~

Why was Jesus not married?

> *Every Avatar adopts a particular aspect of his time. He adapts and embodies his mode of working according to the attitudes of the people.*
>
> *The outstanding weakness that marked the attitude of the people in the time of Jesus was pomp, cruelty, and pride; and to do away with that and set an example, he based his working or mode of life on simplicity, humility, and suffering. And so there was no necessity for him to marry.*
>
> *In the time of Muhammad, lust dominated in the minds of men, so much so that nearly every man used to have sex with several women. Muhammad took note of this, made it lawful for every follower of his to have only a certain number of wives, and himself married seven. Had he, like Jesus, not married, then it would have been deemed essential to make it lawful for his followers to remain unmarried, but nobody in that case would have followed him. It would have been worse than useless to come to nil from numerous, and so he fixed the number to seven from scores.*
>
> *The people were too much steeped in materialism in the age of Buddha; therefore, stressing the nothingness of Maya, he set an example of true renunciation, and left his wife and children. He founded his system on renunciation and sannyas [renunciation of desire].*
>
> *Dry atmosphere marked the age of Krishna. The predominating elements then were internal strife, jealousy, greed. So he preached and founded his teachings on the gospel of love and gaiety, so that people began learning lessons in them and developing love.*
>
> *The hopelessness of the situation in Zoroaster's time, when people progressed neither materially nor spiritually, made him base his system so as to make them live the life of the world, yet be spiritually inclined*

in search of God and Truth. He enacted certain laws and made it incumbent on his followers not to marry more than one woman and not to regard any other with a lustful eye. He founded his religion on the tenets of good thoughts, good words, good deeds.

In reality all these Avatars were the manifestations of the same One Divinity, devoid of desires and above lust, greed, and anger.

Why do the teachings of Avatars vary?

The same One Divine Element had to give different teachings according to the different attitudes of the people in different times and in different circumstances. One forbade the drinking of wine, another smoking. A third advised the worship of a personal God, another advocated impersonal worship. One instituted the worship of God through the medium of different elements of Nature. So, according to the times and circumstances, every Avatar left behind him a different teaching.

For example, there are about twenty to twenty-five patients in a hospital. Those complaining of thirst in the morning are prescribed tea or coffee. Those with the same complaint at noon are given lemon-water; in the evening, buttermilk; and at night, hot milk. The physician is the same, the complaint is the same. But the one complaint [thirst] is satisfied in different ways according to different conditions at different times.

In the same way, God is One, but His manifestations at different times, to satisfy the thirst [for Truth], prescribe different ways and remedies.

What is destiny, luck, fate?

Destiny means the divine will guiding the lines of sin and virtue [resulting in suffering and happiness] experienced by the soul from the beginning of its evolution till its end in Realization.

Fate or luck or fortune is the means or process of spending the impressions that the soul gathers while passing through innumerable evolutionary stages — in other words, the law of karma, or the automatic forming of luck or fate in the next life, according to the sanskaras gathered in this life.

The impressions of every life build the fate of the life coming after. As a simile, suppose every soul has to bear a burden of seven hundred tons [that is, a certain amount of suffering and happiness that every soul has to pass through] from the beginning of its evolution till the end in Realization. But as the burden [of these seven hundred tons] varies in kind and form, the impressions of lives vary too, and the fate or every new life is formed according to the impressions gathered in the past life. Thus the soul's experience of the impressions of the past life means fate. The soul has to pass through a certain number of lives and forms; but as the experiences of every life vary, so does fate also vary.

Hence, destiny is one, but fate [luck or fortune] is different.

~

If all the beautiful things we have known — moonlight, stars, music, the sound of the sea, the fragrance of flowers, our little dreams — are Maya [illusion], what is there left to take their place when you sweep them out of our hearts and minds and leave only the concept of a very far-off and abstract goal of Realization? For until we are realized, it leaves us nothing but emptiness, and very sad.

Beauty and ugliness have relative existence. To one trudging along barefooted under a scorching sun with an empty stomach, Maya outside will not look beautiful. The mood of the subject [the perceiver] invests the object [the perceived] with its own coloring.

The goal of Realization does not necessarily imply for the average man a denial of things good or bad. It only emphasizes their relative worth. From the heights of Realization, Maya would cease to exist; it was pure imagination. Even apart from this experience, the conception that you are in the world but not of the world would go a long way in dissipating sadness and the feeling of void or emptiness.

If one were to treat Maya, sincerely and wholeheartedly, as pure imagination, this external disinterestedness would automatically open up one's internal fountain of bliss, and instead of feeling sad and empty, one would be able to live the perfect life of harmony with the whole universe.

Shall we, who dare not entertain what to us is the presumptuous hope of attaining Realization at this point in our journey, finish this life with none of the small but beautiful things that we as human beings have been used to turning to for solace?

It all depends on whether what you term "solace" is elevating or degrading. Recourse to alcohol for drowning one's sorrows is a perverted form of solace. Solace afforded by things outside of you is synonymous with doping that gives a certain amount of relief or relaxation. Real and unalloyed solace is within you.

It is never presumptuous for anyone to hope for Realization. It is the goal of creation and the birthright of humanity. Blessed are they who are prepared to assert that right in this very life.

Will I have to wait until I have received Realization to carry on work on the astral plane, as I asked when I first met you? Do I work now without being able to bring anything through? How long will it be before I am able direct my consciousness deliberately to leave my body and establish contact with those whom I love, or would like to help, regardless of time and place?

Yes, you are working on the astral plane but unconsciously. In order to do so consciously, you are to attain illumination [sixth plane], which is a prelude to Realization. I have assured you of the experience one day.

Is it impertinent to ask why you are focusing our attention on such a high goal rather than showing us the lower planes and giving us an understanding of their properties and functions? The high ideal is so removed from our understanding that it leaves us empty, dissatisfied, still as blind as ever, like a class of children listening to the nebular theory. Without this more elementary knowledge, how can we go back into the world and answer the questions of those who only need and can understand just a little help to solve these problems? We would seem to be then like hundreds of spiritual teachers whose words go over the heads of the humble seekers. Most of them are too tired or too blind to deal with higher concepts. They need the simple remedies first.

There is no higher or lower goal. There is only one goal —Self-realization. The journey of the planes, from one to the other, is like

changing one prison cell for another, or it amounts to exchanging iron
fetters for gold ones. In neither case is one free, and it is perfect freedom
from the bindings of the physical and the spiritual planes that I aim at.
The advancement on the planes may connote progress and beatitude,
tempting to the wayfarer; but the allurements of a plane once entered
are difficult to shake off. In fact, the bindings [sanskaras] of the physical
plane are much easier to destroy than the bindings of the astral planes.
I wish you to be free once and forever.

What is meant by "turning the key"? And what effect does it have on the
lives of those to whom it is applied?

Perfect Masters as a rule work and bring about results of a spiritual
character in a natural way. On rare but significant occasions, they have
to disregard the natural laws and bring about the desired result by the
use of divine powers. For instance, suppose I want a certain person to
come to me and be with me for his spiritual benefit, and because this is
not possible, owing to the parents' objections to it, the person in question
develops symptoms of leprosy. Seeing this state of affairs, the panicky
parents of their own accord bring the person in question and hand him
over to my charge. This is "turning the key."

Do you want us to accept everything you tell us blindly, whether we
understand it or not, or may we ask questions?

No, I do not want you to accept everything blindly. I like
discrimination and a sense of humor. You may ask questions, but the
most necessary ones.

What are the psychic, mental, and spiritual reactions to preserving silence
as you have done for so long, and in what degree do organizations react
from the same practice over a short period of time?

Universal Mind and Infinite Consciousness have infinite ways of
working universally. So whichever work one does, it reverberates
throughout the universe and produces a reflex action. If the Master
fasts, the result of fasting is felt spiritually by the whole universe.
A Master's work is always for the spiritual end. If he observes silence,
the same result is brought about.

At present the world is laboring under terrible economic chaos.
To follow the spiritual path and to enable the mind to accept the
spiritual, the material needs must be satisfied to a certain extent.
So when I give food and clothing to the poor with my own hands,
the result will be that the world will gain its economic and material
welfare. When I give the mad and lepers a bath, the effect will be
that those of subnormal or abnormal consciousness and the lepers
will either get cured or have their future births lessened.

When I ask any one of you to bathe a leper, your doing it serves a
dual purpose. In the first place, you are trained to tackle difficult work,
which automatically, from the spiritual standpoint, results in the
gradual elimination of your ego, and secondly, the habit of obeying
my orders implicitly and unquestioningly is developed. For example,
if I ask you to observe silence, and if you have the sufficient grounding
in that respect, I can then rely upon you to obey me in other, similar
difficult tasks.

Also, as you are near to me and connected with me, your observance
of fast, silence, or bathing of the lepers will affect the whole range of
your work for me.

You have said that to keep the love of your disciples for you unalloyed,
you must humor the less noble aspects of their nature, such as pride,
jealousy, and so on. How great can their love be if they have to be spiritually
bribed to keep it alive and uppermost? And by fostering the very things
that can be destroyed, how can their progress be speeded up? Doesn't this
hold it back, make it difficult all around?

The love of disciples can never be said to be perfect. The Beloved up to
a point is constrained to humor the lovers [disciples] for the purpose of
drawing them nearer. This nearness to the Beloved in turn fans the fire
of love, which soon achieves perfection and automatically destroys in
the lovers the less noble aspects of their nature.

~

How can I have happiness?

Everyone in the world, consciously or unconsciously, seeks happiness in one form or another. You seek it now in your own way. Even a murderer seeks happiness, which he hopes to find in the very act of murder, and that is why he commits it. Why or when does a man commit murder? Either through hatred or jealousy, and because he thinks he will find happiness if he commits murder and takes his revenge for hatred or jealousy. Why does a man drink? Because of the happiness he derives from the drink. But what happiness does he derive and how long does it last? Only as long as the effect of the intoxication lasts. No sooner does it cool down than he feels broken, dejected, and miserable. It is the same case with lust and lustful actions. One does it all for the happiness one derives even for a moment. But it is only for the moment that one derives happiness from one action or another, and when it is over, he is miserable again.

Real happiness is quite different. It never changes or ceases. It is permanent, everlasting—and it lies there within you. It is sleeping and must be opened. Once it is opened, it is always happiness. I am the source of happiness, the sun of all bliss. But there is a curtain that veils you from the sun, and you do not see it. Now, because of your inability to see owing to a curtain, you cannot say there is no sun. The sun is there, shining and spreading its luster all over the world. But you do not allow its rays to approach you, obstructing them with the veil of ignorance. Remove that, and you will see the sun. I will help you tear open the curtain and enable you to find happiness within. I love you. I love all.

It is through many reverses in life that one learns and finds light. I learned a lot from this, and besides got time for doing Baba's work, which I would not otherwise have got.

It is for your ultimate good…everything else will adjust itself automatically for you. Do not worry, and go on with the work entrusted to you. The light is just behind the apparent darkness. It is because people, out of ignorance, misunderstand and misjudge the "veil" for the darkness and get impatient that they are miserable. Otherwise there is nothing to be miserable about.

Baba, I am intrigued by your ways of working. Could you please explain?

There are three principal ways in which I work:

(1) individually, (2) collectively [for crowds and masses], and (3) universally.

When I work individually, it is with persons (a) who are with me, (b) who are away from me, and (c) who are connected with me. In some cases, I work through their material downfall; in some, through their material welfare. In some cases, I deliberately bring about material downfall, but always keep their spiritual upliftment at heart. In some cases, I use them as "mediums" to efface their own Mayavic qualities, for their own salvation, and that's where I am misunderstood. But I don't mind it; I know why I do it. That is sufficient; because, when love and hatred are in the extreme, both have the same results. For example, A loves me and thinks of nothing but me all the while and is lost in me; whereas B is against me and hates me, but always thinks of me with antagonistic feelings…I always use the medium of thought…it depends upon the qualities that readily respond to the push.

When I work collectively, which is generally in theaters, cinema houses, sporting grounds, and games, where people collect and concentrate on a particular object, it is easy for me to have my spiritual effect on their minds collectively.

When I work universally, it is through agents. Mind, being universal, is linked up with every individual mind…even with advanced minds, who are my agents, and so in every part of the world I am present and working through agents. That is why at times (a) while speaking to one person, my mind is working elsewhere. People have seen me stopping suddenly in the midst of conversation as if absent and away from the spot, engrossed in something else. (b) At night, on many occasions, I make some of my devotees sit beside me and press the soles of my feet. (c) Sometimes, my personal attendant abruptly sits up in his bed at night, noticing some signs or a flash of light, which makes him nervous. At such times, there is special working that pertains to bodiless "spirits" only, who are entering the path of evolution. There are scores of such spirits, but in whatever stage of advancement, they hope to take form again, because the ultimate goal of every soul is to be one with the Infinite, and that is only possible in human form. This is, in short, how I work.

How do the agents know?

Only those who are on the fourth, fifth, sixth, and seventh planes, and who are conscious of me, know under and for whom they are working physically; they have this knowledge through the medium of their subtle and mental bodies. (One in Rishikesh, India, never saw me but knows me.) They cannot see me physically; but because their subtle and mental bodies are detached from the gross, they see my subtle body, which is similar to my gross, and the consciousness of the planes they are in, makes their spirits know the individual behind my subtle body. So they know that they work under me, whose subtle body they see, and which is similar to my physical form. They also know that I am one with the Infinite. For example, while I am sitting here, my agents are working in India, Iran, Africa, and so on. This very moment, they see my subtle body, all at the same time, on different planes, because the messages they send are sent through the mental plane, where there is only the will to do a thing, and instantaneously it reaches the desired spot.

How do they become agents?

Mostly due to past connections with me. Those connected with me in past lives become "agents." Those deeply connected become "members of the Circle."

What is a Circle?

A Circle means those of my deeply connected disciples who are unconsciously one with me now and will consciously be one with me in future, when I have completed the work which I can do during the period of their apparent ignorance. It is like a veil. They are one, but being behind the veil, they do not see. Where love, lover, and Beloved are one, there the work of duality ends. So, for the sake of the work, this duality and ignorance exist. The agents do the work for the people on the gross plane, and through the Circle I work for the spiritual plane, without their [members of the Circle] being aware of it. Jesus worked through his apostles on the spiritual plane without their knowing it;

but later on, they knew it. They knew that all the time, it was Jesus working, and they were his instruments or mediums, and were all the time one with Jesus. For example, you as W are one. W is in your hands, eyes, ears, and feelings. Now, if W wants to help N or K, he uses his legs to make him stand up, his eyes to see, his hands to strike. All these—hands, eyes, ears—are one body, but made to work separately and individually for different work, at different times, in different circumstances.

Many people accuse you of mass hypnotism. Can you explain?

In mass hypnotism by others, the effect on the masses is temporary, but my effect on them is permanent. In mass hypnotism by others, the effect is on the mind; but in my working, it is the soul that is affected and advanced. There are certain yogis in India who, for their self-interest, hypnotize the minds of people coming in their contact, and get their objective fulfilled. What happens? People whose minds are hypnotized, after being free from the temporary effects, neither gain nor lose spiritually, even if, during hypnotism, they are made to commit the worst of sins or crimes. Their spiritual position, however, remains the same. Once, in the time of Janak [a king of ancient times], there was an incident. He had many enemies, and their ring leader was one who was loved by Janak's courtiers. Janak wanted these very courtiers, who loved his enemy, to kill him. So he sought the aid of a yogi and told him what he wanted. This yogi had great powers. He summoned the courtiers, about ten of them, hypnotized and influenced them to such an extent that they went and killed the enemy [of the state] whom they loved. Later, after the deed was done and the influence wore off, they repented for having killed one whom they loved. What I want to point out is that for this action, even that of killing a man, they [those hypnotized] are not responsible. Their spiritual position remains the same. My spiritual influence is permanent. It is on a person's life, body, mind, and soul; in short, on everything.

Meher Baba is fond of children.

Yes, I am but a child. Not until one becomes a child does one achieve the slightest spiritual experience. When one becomes a child, one enjoys bliss. Nothing worries him — thoughts, words, or actions.

[A merchant introduces a moneylender to Baba, with an apologetic explanation that the moneylender, unlike his professional brothers, is spiritual.]

[Addressing the moneylender] When your mind is inclined to spirituality, it does not matter what line of work you are in.

Can anyone get self-realization all of a sudden, or does it come only through gradual spiritual progress and experience?

In some cases, self-realization occurs all at once, as in my case. In other cases, experience culminates in Realization gradually.

What is Infinity?

That which is contained in your own self.

Can the finite mind realize the Infinite?

There is nothing like finite. Even now, when you think that you are finite, your conception of finite is not real. There is nothing like finite. As long as the sense of binding remains, one can only have mere glimpses of the Infinite, but when the Infinite is realized, it is found that the finite was the Infinite all the time. So there is no question of the finite finding the Infinite.

Is it due to ignorance that the finite does not know that it is Infinite?

Yes, but this ignorance is the medium for the self to realize the Self. And self-realization means knowledge. Just as a bird that is always free does not know that it is free, but when it is imprisoned in a cage and then set free, then it knows what freedom is. And just as this impression of its imprisonment has been the medium for the bird's knowing and appreciating "freedom," so also, although you are all-knowledge all the while, you do not know that you are all-knowledge; and your present

ignorance, like the bird's imprisonment, is the medium that will help
you to comprehend that you are all-knowledge all along.

What is the cause of ignorance?

The cause of individual ignorance is the result of evolutionary
impressions; and the collective ignorance is the outcome of the very
first existence. All is Infinite. In self-realization, there is no finite; but
as long as you are not individually free from duality, duality exists for
you. The substratum of all this is love. Love is the one and only thing.
Devoid of love, everything is miserable. Love is God and everything
that is real. Lust is perverted love, and so it is unreal.

Is this your message to us?

Yes, for you and also for the whole world.

~

Is decent living enough for attaining a wider consciousness, or is any
occult, spiritual, or religious training necessary?

No general rule or process can be laid down for the attainment of
the ultimate reality or, as you term it, "wider consciousness." Every
individual has got to work out his own salvation, and for that matter,
he himself has got to create and choose the "path," which is mostly
determined and expressed by the collective force and momentum of
impressions [sanskaras] acquired during previous lives. The panacea
the world knows of, the so-called religions for the guidance of humanity,
do not go a long way in solving the problem. As time goes on, the founder,
the one who provided the motivating force, is thrown and relegated
more and more into the background of time and obscurity. In the
aftermath of his manifestations, either a religion or an organization
gradually loses its glamor and attractiveness, and a mental revolt takes
place against the old order of things. A demand is created for
something more tangible, substantial, and practical, through which
one may learn to live the true life, the life of the spirit; and you know
that supply is in proportion to demand. To say that only "decent
living" is the way of attaining "wider consciousness" is to give only one

side of the picture. What you are today is the result of your decent and indecent living as well. Occult, spiritual, and religious training serves merely as means to an end and is a condition precedent to entering the Path; but the moment one has the contact of a Perfect Master, no such disciplinary process is necessary. The only thing required is complete surrenderance to his supreme will and unquestioning willingness and attitude of mind to suffer and accept things as they come.

What spiritual work do you suggest for modern Europe?

There exists at the moment a universal dissatisfaction and an indescribable longing for something that will end this terrible chaos and misery that is startling the world. I am going to satisfy this craving and lead the world to real happiness and peace by making mankind become more introspective and see more to the inside of things than what they have hitherto been accustomed to.

Do you help individually or collectively?

As a rule, Masters help individually according to the temperament and preparedness of the aspirant, but this being the Avataric period — the end of the previous cycle and the beginning of a new one, which occurs every seven or eight hundred years — my spiritual help to humanity will be both individual and collective. The period of junction of the old and new cycle usually connotes the advent of a Master who rejuvenates and infuses new life and meaning into the old order of things, and besides imparting to the select few the highest state of spirituality — the state of oneness with the infinite ocean of bliss, knowledge, and power — a general spiritual push is given to the whole universe.

Do you think a possible spiritual revival will be the outcome of individual effort, or rather a collective movement of nations (like the great religious movements in the past)? Will certain nations achieve it sooner than others?

The spiritual revival that you ask about is not very far off, and I am going to bring it about in the near future, utilizing the tremendous amount of misapplied energy possessed by America for the purpose. Such a spiritual outburst that I visualize takes place every seven or

eight hundred years, at the end or beginning of a cycle, and it is only
the Perfect One, who has reached the Christ state of consciousness,
that can work so very universally.

Will you deal with such problems as politics, economics, and sex?
My working will embrace everything; it will affect and control every
phase of life. Perfection would fall far short of the ideal if it were to
accept one thing and eschew another. In the general spiritual push that
I shall impart to the world, problems such as politics, economics, and
sex, although they have no direct connection with the original theme,
will all be automatically solved and adopted; and new values and
significance will be attached to matters that appear to baffle people at
this time. All collective movements and religions hinge around one
personality, for without this centrifugal force, all movements are
bound to fail. Societies and organizations have never succeeded in
bringing the truth nearer. Perfect Masters impart spirituality by
personal contact and influence, and the benefit that will accrue to
different nations, when I bring about the spiritual upheaval, will
largely depend upon the amount of energy each one possesses. The
more the energy, however misapplied, the greater the response; the
Master merely diverts the current in the right direction.

How can one get away from material things if one is forced by one's
nature to put the main accent in life on them?
I don't believe in external renunciation, and for the West particularly,
it is impractical and inadvisable. Renunciation should be mental. One
should live in the world, perform all legitimate duties, and yet feel
mentally detached from everything; one should be in the world but not
of the world.

Why does one talk in connection with you of "performing miracles"?
Don't you think this may lead people into the most "materialistic" and
cheapest kind of belief?
In the West I find people very keen on the question of miracles. I
must explain that the ability to perform miracles does not necessarily
connote high spirituality. Anyone who has attained perfection and

enjoys the Christ-consciousness can perform miracles. Healing the sick, giving eyes to the blind, or raising the dead to life is mere child's play to him. Even those who have not become one with the Infinite, but are only traversing the planes, can perform miracles and are able to do and undo things. It is not, however, to be understood that spiritual masters perform miracles to order just to satisfy idle curiosity. Miracles have come to be performed, and will be performed, according to existing circumstances. Masters have sometimes performed miracles when it is intended to give a universal push towards spirituality. I shall give a universal push towards spirituality. I shall perform miracles when the time and situation demand it and not for mere sensation mongering.

Have you been in touch with other Masters only spiritually or even in physical contact?

Yes, I have been in touch with spiritual masters, even physically, before realization. It is almost impossible to achieve the highest state of consciousness without a Master. It was the physical contact of my master Hazrat Babajan of Poona, a single kiss on my forehead, that gave me the consciousness I now eternally enjoy. I now take orders from no one; it is all my supreme will. Everything is, because I will it to be. Nothing is beyond my knowledge; I am in everything. There is no time and space for me. It is I who give them their relative existence. I see the past and the future as clearly and vividly as you see material things about you.

I feel extremely grateful for this privilege of being allowed to meet you. I have been in India for years, and I feel I belong to India. Do you feel so too, Baba?

Yes.

Do you think I shall have to go there again in my life?

Yes, you will have to go to the mountains in the later years of your life.

In India?

Yes.

Oh, how wonderful.

And remember what I am telling you now. Don't bind yourself to anything — to any movement or individual — not even to those whom you help. Don't make them too dependent on you so as not to allow you to leave them. This is my special advice.

I will, I will abide by it, gratefully. And now, Baba, what do you think one should do to gain inner peace and advance on the Path? Can one progress in a busy city and life spent therein?

Truly speaking, it does not matter where one lives. It matters how one lives. One can make no progress at all, even if one lives in mountains or caves, if one's mind is engrossed in worldly Maya, while on the other hand, one living in the world, doing all his duties therein, can still achieve much if he is not engrossed in Maya and thinks of the Path. So you could go on with all the good work you have been doing here in the world, but have the same longing for inner life and progress in your heart.

Have you met Annie Besant?

No, but I know her. She is an advanced soul.

I know her since I was a child. They all started it [the Theosophy movement] with good ideas, but too much of "schism" and "personality" spoiled it. And there are so many divisions now.

That's the trouble. In spirituality, it is the heart that counts and not the head. Too much intellectual discourse undermines the object with which these [movements and institutions] are started. So you may go on with the good work that you are doing, and keep your connection with the movements [organizations], but don't be bound to anyone or anything. Keep yourself free.

I am doing work for the last several years, helping the poor and needy.

Good work, but you have still much farther to go. So I tell you, again, don't bind yourself to anything.

I understand. Thank you, Baba, for your kind words and advice. I will do my work, but keep myself free as you say. Is there anything you could give me to do?

Yes. [Baba gives her a certain thought process for daily practice.]

And do I continue my usual daily meditation?

Yes, but this is special. You will feel my help.

Does this mean you accept me?

Yes.

~

What is the solution to this worldwide misery? Would it be solved through martyrdom?

Yes, through martyrdom by many. But why a question of collective efforts for many? What about you personally?

I am not concerned about me personally.

But the personal question does come in, even with a desire to serve others selflessly, as you do, because your personal efforts for the good of others would have a collective effect. For example, a leper amongst a crowd of healthy people would spoil the entire atmosphere and surroundings with the infection of his disease. So also, another emitting perfume from his person would spread the fragrance all around him. That is, personal means collective, and collective means personal. So in order to be able to help others, you yourself must first have it [the knowledge and power]. You can then better transmit this happiness to others.

In spite of keeping one's "personal" question aside, trying one's utmost to help one's own, if they do not understand, what does one do?

So it means the feeling of happiness is not so deep in them as in you. I saw your family, but the happiness you experience is not experienced by them all. And it is the lifelong aim of every true soul to impart happiness to others, even if it is at the sacrifice of one's own.

Perhaps one who is not always encouraged by circumstances feels dejected at times.

But it gradually expands. You have a good heart. I like you very much. Every human being has some weakness. But it is the heart that matters.

How is selfishness caused, and why?

At the root of all is selfishness, self-interest, want, desire. If two dogs see a bone, they fight because they both want it. Both have a desire to possess it. Even if they do not see and do not fight, all the same, the desire is latent there.

Is there fear?

Why do people fear? Because they are afraid of losing the thing they want to possess.

What are the means to be fearless?

The only possible means is the spiritual change of heart. That only will make people satisfied. They want to be "satisfied." They themselves do not know what they want. When they get that, they will be satisfied. For instance, why do people drink? Those who labor hard all day, when they come home after the day's work, drink for stimulation. If they get something else instead, they would be satisfied with that, and so on, until the desire for stimulation disappears. So for all material satisfaction created through desire and want, spiritual upliftment is needed.

But how could spiritual upliftment come when selfishness and desire are so very deeply rooted?

And that will be done by universal love. Love has such powers as to unite all hearts. So the first spiritual universal push will be through love.

What are the hours and time when you concentrate on spiritual work?

There is no fixed time. I do it when I feel like doing. It is Infinite. There is no limitation for the Infinite.

⁓

Is life a battle?

Yes, it is a battle and, if rightly fought, would bring infinite anand [bliss].

Why should it be a battle?

Necessarily, otherwise existence would be a drag. If there is no darkness, one cannot appreciate light; if there is no ignorance, one cannot appreciate knowledge — they can't exist without the other. Both are essential on the opposite poles.

Why is there so much evil in the world?

It is as one takes it. In reality there is nothing but God, good, and bliss, but because of ignorance man doesn't see it and takes the different degrees of expressions of good as evil. Even so, it is essential for the eradication of duality. Passing through different phases and experiences of this duality, man evolves in consciousness and understanding of the one Reality — which alone exists.

But what I mean to say is that there are certain periods when this evil is at its height, and people who were eager to know Truth and were trying to find it do not understand why evil should spread throughout the world to such an alarming extent.

These are real periods which clearly show signs of the real turning point approaching. When evil predominates, it is a sure sign of the good that is coming. It must rise to its highest before it is eradicated and destroyed, root and branch. The various signs of evil all over the world are preceding an era of good that is to immediately follow.

Do you think it will lead to that?

Sure. It will and must. It is a law, the law of duality — good and evil, light and dark, knowledge and ignorance — two forces working in opposites for the attainment of unity. And there are always good souls who help humanity through their good thoughts, words, and actions.

But they are few.

Yes, but these few do a great deal in helping humanity through these good thoughts and acts. And at certain times, leaders do appear for the salvation of humanity. Such a time is approaching, and the world will find its leader that it now seeks.

Do you accept the principle that science and religion are separate?
It depends upon how it is understood. Science, if it deals only with material advancement, would be said to have nothing of spirituality. But when the same science is expressed to make the meaning of life clear, then it is also a branch of spirituality; just as art, if expressed rightly, is spiritual, and if expressed wrongly, is material.

Are scientific truths and principles to be fitted in with spiritual doctrines?
They can be fitted in. What is the gross world, after all, but the medium to realize spirituality? For example, the body is purely material, physical, and gross, but it is the medium for the soul to know itself, provided it is dealt with and handled rightly, otherwise it becomes a hindrance in spiritual progress. Similarly, scientific principles and truths, if used rightly, help in the spiritual progress of the universe, but if improper use is made of them, they are bound to be the source of hindrance on the spiritual path.

Has astrology anything to do with spirituality? Can astrological problems be proved as scientific problems?
Everything has something to do with spirituality; it only depends upon how it is worked out, and that again results in advancing or retarding spiritual progress. Science is a mass thing, while astrology is individual, so science itself cannot be proved to be wrong, while astrology can be proved to be wrong. If a truth is established scientifically, you do not think of doubting it. It does not occur to you to doubt it. If you are told that the earth is round and if it is proved to you, you never think that it is flat. But if an astrologer tells you that you will get a million rupees after some time, you will think of it a million times. Spirituality has no room for doubts. For example, if someone were to ask me, "Are you sure you are one with God?" I would ask him, "Are you sure you are a man and not a dog?" He would say that he is a man because he cannot think of himself as anything but a man. In the same way, I am equally

sure that I am one with God. Even if the whole world tells me otherwise, I do not feel anything about it. Spiritual surety is something that nothing affects.

Is it impossible to understand spiritual matters intellectually?

Spiritual doctrine can be stated in intellectual terms. Intellect is a great help in the experience of the heart. If someone who never had a headache asks you to explain it to him, you will try to explain intellectually what it is. But to make him understand it, you would have to hit him on the head. He gets a headache and knows what it is. There is nothing irrational in spirituality. Christ said, "Leave all and follow me." It means "Leave your limitations and live my life." He meant that it was the practical way. Mysticism is thought to be something supernatural and out of human grasp. It is not so. You may be doing all your worldly duties and at the same time be a mystic. It depends on how you arrange your actions and how you lead a proper life.

Is Mahatma Gandhi a mystic?

He is a mystic in a way. Everyone is a mystic in his or her own way. A real mystical life is practical for everyone who leads life properly. Mysticism has a connection with every phase of life if properly expressed; if not, there is a reaction that cannot be called mysticism. Thus, love, when handled badly through jealousy, is converted into hatred. Mysticism, if adjusted rightly, can help all nations now at war, while if handled otherwise, it would make matters worse. Mysticism means experience of the soul on higher planes. God, the Highest, is attained through this experience.

Is material adjustment amongst nations practical to bring about peace?

Material adjustment can be made with spiritual understanding. If people are made to realize that all the trouble is due to self-interest, then automatically material adjustment will follow.

Is economic adjustment possible so long as human beings are what they are?

Economic adjustment and human nature are interdependent. If it is realized that the trouble is due to self-interest, the problem will be solved. It is easy and simple, yet because of its simplicity, the task is also difficult. For example, if praise and insult did not affect you, you would be always happy. If not, you are bound to be unhappy. How easy the remedy is, yet the simplicity itself makes it difficult.

∽

Is faith in God essential?

That depends on how you interpret faith. Some who have faith and believe in God lead a life without character and fail to make any spiritual progress, while there are others who do not even believe in God but lead such a noble life that they automatically come closer to God.

What is the goal of creation?

To know the self as Infinite Eternal Existence and to enable others to realize this same self.

How did the universe come about?

Universe, if understood as created, has an entirely different meaning from our viewpoint that universe does not exist. Actually it is only God who appears as the universe. But it is necessary for creation to have this dual idea of God and universe.

Why do forces of evil predominate over forces of virtue?

It is all in the scope of universal law. The suffering that appears so grave is necessary for happiness, just as binding is necessary to experience freedom. Unless evil temporarily triumphs, happiness cannot be experienced. This universe is based on duality. Binding and freedom, good and bad, evil and virtue, are interdependent. If only one aspect existed, there would be no interest or meaning in life. For the attainment of ultimate freedom and happiness, temporary victory of evil over virtue is necessary.

Why does God, who is so kind and merciful, give suffering and pain to so many?

God has nothing to do with this. God is all one-in-one. He is aloof and yet so attached that whatever is done is by His law of love and will. For example, when you sleep, you enjoy a dream, and the enjoyment is so intense that this dream of happiness does not wake you soon. But if in the midst of the dream you suddenly saw a snake, you would wake up at once. This is the law of God. God is neither merciful nor cruel in your "awakened" state. To know the exact meaning of the "awake state," one has to experience the "dream state." Dreams can be good and bad. In dreams you can suffer or enjoy. But when you wake up, you find it is all a dream. But this dream should be so adjusted that it awakens you. Sacrifice, character, and selfless service help in awakening you.

Is renunciation of the world necessary for spiritual attainment?

Internal renunciation is necessary, but not external renunciation. It is not the outward escape from the world that leads you to God. You have to live in the world, do all your duties, and yet feel as detached as if you were living in seclusion in the midst of intense activity. How can you renounce this body and mind by retiring into the jungles?

In a country like India, is it not the duty of every Indian to work for the liberation of his country?

Yes, but the aspect must be from a spiritual standpoint. If material freedom binds you to Maya and leads to spiritual avoidance, it is no freedom. You must try heart and soul to have India free, but it must be the freedom that helps you towards Truth and spirituality.

Will India come in the forefront, as in the days of old, to lead the world?

It is the duty of India to lead the world spiritually.

Is the path shown by Mahatma Gandhi the only path to attain India's freedom?

In some respects it is. It depends on the circumstances. If India were not so disunited internally as it is now, the policy of Gandhi would bring freedom in a few moments, but it is so difficult for the Hindus and Muslims to unite. Gandhi saw me four times, and I said the same thing to him — that unless the hearts of Hindus and Muslims are united, little progress can be expected. Work with all your heart, with the one motive of making India truly free, but do not think of the results of your work. Men like you can do what millions cannot do, as you have heart, intellect, and sincerity. This selfless service of yours in striving for India's freedom will lead you ultimately to God.

~

It has been said that by breaking through the different hindrances of lust, hate, and so on, one can develop true love. But your teaching is that by developing true love, one can break through these hindrances.

The method of love is direct. The other method is indirect and round-about. It is like reaching the mouth [for eating] with your hand from behind the neck.

It has been said that a person can, by increasing his own intensity of awareness and effort, break through his bonds and attain freedom. If one can thus free himself, why is a Master necessary?

How can you free yourself when your hands and feet are bound? I can set you free because I am free. If you think that by relying upon yourself you can attain the Truth, you depend upon a teaching. But then why not rely upon the ocean of Truth — the living embodiment of Truth, rather than a dead formula or principle?

When a young aspirant meets young women, he is susceptible to thoughts of lust. On the other hand, if he avoids them entirely, he is likely to withhold a great deal of love. Is there any way out of this dilemma?

Free mixing of the sexes, as in the West, is on the whole good, but if the aspirant feels within his mind the slightest flutter of impure thoughts, he should stand aside. But he must love, and in order to avoid impure thoughts, he should keep in his mind the thought that in the other person he is loving the Master.

The aspirant must undoubtedly eliminate lust and release love. But lust as well as love is a fact of inner life and cannot be taken as being identical with any specific acts of the physical body. Will the aspirant be wrong if he tries to express and develop love [instead of lust] through sex union?

If the aspirant thinks that through the sex act he is expressing love, he is mistaken. It is lust that prompts him to it. It is not possible to express pure love through the sex act because of the clash of impressions involved therein.

What is your teaching concerning marriage?

For an aspirant, celibacy is better than marriage. But if he cannot control himself, he should marry. To pursue a spiritual life, it is much better to marry than to go from flower to flower.

How can the aspirant use marriage for spiritual progress?

In the beginning the aspirant will, in relation to the partner, feel lust as well as love. But he can, with conscious and deliberate cooperation with the partner, gradually lessen the element of lust and increase the element of love, until love becomes utterly pure and free from lust. But in order to achieve this purpose, he must strictly limit himself to his partner in matters of sex.

⤳

Is it not difficult for you to express yourself clearly in your high mission and noble undertaking?

No, because both mediums, internal and external, are at my disposal.

Have you concentrated your attention on the upliftment of Zoroastrians?

I am actually working for universal upliftment, which includes Zoroastrians.

Are you not annoyed by press representatives at home and abroad?

Never annoyed with anything or anyone.

Have you any political aim besides a religious one?

Spirituality embraces religion, politics, social matters, etc.

What are the reasons of the present financial depression?

Self-interest is the reason for financial depression, which will pass away in future.

What is your line of work?

Love and Service.

Are you of the opinion that the present civilization is degrading humanity?

No. That which degrades is no civilization.

Do you take trouble to be in contact with political developments of India and of other Western countries?

Of every department of life, of every nation.

Is it true that foreign countries like America and England are in a position to supply the world with industrial education that has so much accounted for their prosperity in the long run, but failed to produce effect this time [in 1933]?

The West can teach material things to the East, and the East can teach spiritual things to the West.

[After overcoming a little nervousness, an elderly man questions Baba about the main "turning point" in his life, which, he felt, had arisen, even at the age of about sixty, after so many minor failures he had experienced in life.]

The turning point has to arrive in the life of everyone, as it has arrived in your case now. It is like a war. Every day, every hour, and every minute of man's life is a sort of a minor war between mind and heart, emotion and intellect, good and bad. And when these individual conflicts spread out and develop, the collective result eventually takes the shape of a big worldwide war, which can never be avoided by any number of peace conferences, unless and until the very root cause is removed.

Shall I continue to do what I am doing now?

> *Yes. It is all right. Only if you do it with confidence, but whatever one does with confidence has the desired result. Even things that are apparently bad, if done with the right motive, bear good results, because in that very action, selflessness exists.*

∼

How to be a true Christian?

> *By following the teachings of Christ, by living the life that he lived and wanted you to live. People talk of Christianity but are not prepared to follow Christ's words "to turn the other cheek," saying it is "impractical," and fly at one another's throat at the slightest provocation, creating hatred, when Jesus wanted them to create an atmosphere of love and brotherhood everywhere. No wonder the world is in a muddle about everything.*

I am concerned about the grave crisis coming in the near future and wish to ask you whether there is going to be another war.

> *Yes, there will be another war…and what a war! But it will be nothing but a turning point. Before the major turning point there are minor turning points. For example, take war. Before the actual war between nations with arms and ammunitions on a large, worldwide scale takes place in the near future, people have minor wars to undergo—a conflict between mind and heart, emotion and intellect, good and evil, also economic wars all over—all these gradually growing to such an extent as to develop into a great, major war, like the last world war [World War I]. And rest assured, there will be one in the future.*

And that will demand my duty towards my country. Shall I stick to it?

> *Yes. Duty always stands first, whatever it is. And the very feeling and desire for duty means spirituality, because it is selflessness and sincerity of heart that call for duty.*

*[The answers given by Baba seem to please the interviewer very much. He asks for Baba's help, and Baba says: **I will help you spiritually**.]*

~

[A questioner speaks of the conflict between emotion and discretion.]
When the intellect discards the dictates of conscience, or when the
heart does not respond to what the intellect says, there is disharmony.
So discretion and emotion must go hand in hand. In every phase of
life, material and spiritual, this is true. If you accept a thing without
discretion, and later on repent for it, there is disharmony. Similarly, if
you don't accept a thing through prejudice, and later on find you ought
to have accepted it, there is disharmony. People seem to seek happiness,
but they make it so complicated that they become disgusted with it. Yet
it is so simple. If discretion [head] and emotion [heart] act together, it
is better. But if preference is to be given spiritually, it is first to the
conscience. If your heart says it is right to love God in everyday life,
and your intellect says it is not wrong, you are to decide immediately
to act in preference to your heart. Real happiness is within. Once you
know how to attain it, you will find it everywhere.

~

If you are the Christ, why do people not know?
It is because people cannot know that I have to take this human form.
Jesus was not known in his time, even by his own intimate and
immediate companions. Judas, who was all the time near him and
kissed him, could not understand him. So you too do not understand
me externally in my physical form, because as the Real, Infinite Christ,
I am within you, as in everybody.

If God is in everything, why is this evil prevalent in the world...this sort
of "disproportion"?
God is One, Infinite, and as you now said, is in everything. But this
good and evil, virtue and vice, suffering and happiness, are all apparent,
and not real. It is a delusion; and yet it is necessary and serves its
purpose. It is through this duality of good and evil that one has to
realize oneness. This duality is the medium, because, in reality, bad is
not bad as you think. It is a degree of goodness. For instance, love and

hatred, though opposite in terms, when carried to the extreme, both have the same result. You are surprised, but I will explain. Suppose, A loves me very much. It means he thinks continually of nothing else but of me and is perfectly lost in me. Now, there is B, who hates me. His extreme hatred makes him think of me always, and he is continually absorbed in me and thinks of me. Thus, love and hatred, though poles apart apparently, have the same result in their extremes. So this duality of good and evil are necessary to know what oneness is. A bird, free from its very birth and never caged, does not know what freedom really is, because it has always been free, that is, in the same condition from its very birth. If it is once caged, that is, the condition reversed, and left free again later on, then alone will it know and appreciate the value and meaning of "freedom." The cage therefore becomes the medium for the bird to realize freedom.

Why all this misconception about "duality" in all things?

It is not misconception, because in reality, only one exists. What appears as two is delusion due to ignorance. Once this delusion about the apparent duality of all things disappears, there remains nothing but the One Infinite Existence. You are perfect, but you are not conscious of it, due to the darkness of ignorance. Yet this apparent ignorance is the necessary process to get that consciousness of perfection. Realize the one indivisible unity everywhere and in everything, and help others. Everyone is Christ, but very few can become Jesus.

∽

Very, very happy to meet you.

So am I.

How kind of you to come all this way from India.

This is my work, and I am pleased to meet true, sincere, and loving souls here.

I have felt for a long time that India has much to give to the West.

India is a land of spiritual birth.

But the West is practical, which is essential too, I believe.
Life would be ideal if India's spiritual mind would be put together with the practical mind of the West.

I would love to visit India and see you there.
You will, one day.

～

I am sorry, Baba, for all this, but you know I couldn't help it and was afraid I would miss seeing you, being so late. It is such a privilege to see you. I met Krishnamurti once. He took off what I didn't need, but could give me nothing instead, so that I felt quite empty after I left him, with no interest in life.
It is all there in you, waiting to be unlocked.

The East is mystical, the West practical.
The practical mind of the West and the mystical mind of the East must go hand in hand. Then only is the real balance of the head and heart achieved.

And when will that be?
Soon. There has been a marked awakening in the West for the inner life and Truth, and the time will soon come when the world will know the real value and purpose of life.

I felt that life was a mathematical problem, dry, cold, and shallow, with nothing real, substantial, and deep inside.
Let me explain. Truth is not to be intellectually understood, but is to be felt, experienced, and realized. And for that, no intellectual gymnastics or logical arguments are necessary, but a clean, open, receptive heart that accepts what is given and poured in.

Yes, Baba, I now understand. But how could I achieve it, receive it?
I will give it to you.

Oh, how grateful!

[Here Baba gives her a certain thought to meditate on with his explanation of the process of how to do it, avoiding the pitfalls. She is so pleased with the central thought given her for meditation that she exclaims, "How wonderful," in an ecstatic mood. And when Baba says, **You will feel my help**, *tears fill her eyes and trickle down her cheeks.]*

~

I am trying to realize the greater things in life, but find it extremely difficult to reconcile myself with the surroundings, which are all so material and to which I feel so apathetic.

It is all right if you feel that way.

And should I still continue doing it, even if I think it is not right?

You need not worry if you feel the way you do outside the world of matter. And even while living with others and doing things as they like, if you feel within that it is all wrong, it is splendid. Let me explain. In India there are places like the Himalayas where the rishis [sages], ascetics, and mystics retire in seclusion, to be away from the world and meditate for years. But after years of such secluded life in the mountains and caves, when they return to the world, they find it very difficult to adjust themselves to its surroundings, and in many cases there is a reaction. In the West it is different. Yet there are sincere souls here, too, who seek Truth. There is an awakening even in the West. But it is difficult to reconcile the two—material and spiritual living. I know how you feel. You shouldn't feel disappointed with this situation or conflict. You must always remember that in spirituality it is not the intellect and external life that matter, but it is the feelings and inner experiences that count. You can live in the world, do all your duties, and yet be spiritual. You shouldn't run away from the world nor shirk your duties, but live in the world doing all your legitimate duties, keeping your mind always towards the goal.

Oh, I didn't know that. I thank you for your advice. I thought I was mistaken in living a life I didn't want to and was puzzled. You know it is so difficult to live with people, even with the family who do not understand; and out of their regard for me, they all persuade me to live a life of ease and comfort that they live, but which I know and feel is not real. We must suffer, and yet I have to do it all for them, though all the while I feel it is wrong.

I understand, and as I have already told you, it is quite all right that you feel that way. The external life doesn't matter if you feel differently internally. So don't worry about this inner conflict. You will be helped. This contact will help you.

Thank you, Baba, I think it will. Is there anything you think I should do?
Do you ever meditate?

Yes, I do.
Then do one thing...
[Baba gives her a certain thought to meditate on, explaining the simple process of doing it, avoiding all the hard and stiff methods and strain of yoga practices and helping her do it in a relaxed position, but sincerely.]
You will be helped.

One who has a living in the world has to look out for the necessities of life, and in the pursuit of that misses something that is behind it all. For instance, a man of my type, who has to work with the outside world of matter, has to adjust to their way of living in despite my desire to attain to something substantial behind all this, which from my little reading and knowledge I know others have achieved. But I am afraid also to take a jump right at the top of a mountain [meaning by this to take great strides on the Path].

I understand. You mean "spirituality made practical."

Yes, that is it exactly, to put it in short.
And it is very easy, very simple. Its very simplicity makes it difficult.

Is it really? How strange!

People's ideas about God and spirituality are so far-fetched, fantastic, and funny.

You see, Baba, I call my highest ideal the "Life Substance." I don't want to call it God, for that would be connected with the rigid church diction and dogmas, even though my belief and ideal would be greater.

Names and terms do not matter. It is the feeling that counts.

Then what should I do to feel and get a glimpse of it, if not get deeper into it?

I will explain. For a man of your position in life, in a civilized country like America, it is all right to live a life as you do, keeping your mind always towards higher aspirations. To speak frankly, you are spiritual without being conscious of it.

Am I really?

Yes, I know you really are more spiritual than you know yourself. But you could do much more.

And what must I do to get deeper into it and gain greater knowledge? Can you tell me anything?

Yes, I will. And as I told you already, it is very simple. One must do it.

I would be delighted. [Baba gives him a certain thought and explains to him how to concentrate on it.] And may I think of you? Would it be all right?

Yes, do. I will help you.

I am so grateful, grateful for the privilege of this meeting, for the very interesting talk, and for the invaluable help given.